AMERICA The BEAUTIFUL

OHIO

By Deborah Kent

Consultants

Shirley Smith Seaton, Ph.D., former Directing Supervisor of Social Studies, Cleveland Public Schools

John J. Grabowski, Ph.D., Curator of Manuscripts, Western Reserve Historical Society

Robert L. Hillerich, Ph.D., Bowling Green State University

 CHILDRENS PRESS®

CHICAGO

Autumn in Holmes County

Project Editor: Joan Downing
Associate Editor: Shari Joffe
Design Director: Margrit Fiddle
Typesetting: Graphic Connections, Inc.
Engraving: Liberty Photoengraving

Library of Congress Cataloging-in-Publication Data

Kent, Deborah.
  America the beautiful. Ohio / by Deborah Kent.
    p.   cm.
  Includes index.
  Summary: Introduces the geography, history,
government, economy, industry, culture, historic
sites, and famous people of this diverse
midwestern state.
    ISBN 0-516-00481-6
    1. Ohio—Juvenile
literature. [1. Ohio] I. Title.
F491.3.K46 1989   88-38401
977.1—dc19   CIP
                                            AC

The Cleveland skyline along the Cuyahoga River

TABLE OF CONTENTS

Chapter 1
WHERE ALL THINGS
ARE POSSIBLE

WHERE ALL THINGS ARE POSSIBLE

For nearly 150 years, the people of Ohio tried to find a motto that could represent their state. Briefly, during the 1860s, the state adopted the solemn Latin phrase *Imperium in Imperio*, meaning "an empire within an empire." But after two years, the practical Ohioans rejected this scholarly slogan and began their search once more.

Ohio is a state of lush forests and bubbling creeks. Rich veins of coal and deposits of marble, limestone, and salt lie beneath the earth's surface. Charming small towns are scattered amid endlessly rolling farmland, while factories in teeming cities turn out steel, chemicals, plastics, and gasoline. On Lake Erie and along the Ohio River, huge ships take on cargo destined for ports around the world. Ohio has produced presidents, inventors, authors, and astronauts. It is home to people whose lives are grounded in the soil and the seasons, as well as to people who thrive on the uncertain turns of industry and finance. How could a few words capture the essence of this state, which is so many things to so many people?

In 1959, still searching for a motto, the state legislature turned for help to Ohio's schoolchildren, asking them for their suggestions. A twelve-year-old boy from Cincinnati, James Mastranardo, found a line in the Bible that conveyed all that Ohio is today, and everything it may become in the years ahead. The legislature accepted James's slogan as the state's official motto: With God, All Things Are Possible.

Chapter 2

THE LAND

THE LAND

TOPOGRAPHY

Ohio lies along the eastern edge of the broad, flat, fertile region known as the Midwest. Perfectly straight surveyors' lines mark the borders with Pennsylvania to the east, Indiana to the west, and Michigan at the northwestern corner. The shore of Lake Erie outlines about three-fourths of the state's northern boundary. In the south, the winding arc of the Ohio River separates the state from Kentucky and West Virginia. Ohio ranks thirty-fifth in size among the states, with an area of 41,330 square miles (107,045 square kilometers).

About 500 million years ago, a shallow, inland sea covered much of the Midwest, including the land that is now Ohio. The seashore was seldom stable. Over millions of years, the water ebbed away and crept forward again and again. When the sea receded for the last time, it left behind a thick deposit of sandstone, shale, and limestone as its legacy. Vast swamps, lush with vegetation, sprawled over the abandoned ocean bed. The decayed remains of this ancient plant life form Ohio's reserves of fossil fuel—coal and oil.

Grooves cut into the rocks on Kelleys Island (left) were carved by glaciers that moved through Ohio thousands of years ago. Shell limestone (above), found throughout Ohio, is the legacy of the inland sea that once covered much of the Midwest.

Between ten thousand and twenty thousand years ago, a series of immense ice sheets, or glaciers, ground their way south from the Arctic. The glaciers covered nearly two-thirds of Ohio's land, grinding and churning the surface as they moved over it. The glaciers carved out three major land regions in Ohio. They gouged out the bed of Lake Erie, the shallowest of the Great Lakes, and left a strip of fertile lowland called the Great Lakes Plain along Lake Erie's shore. In the northwest part of the state, the Great Lakes Plain is more than fifty miles (eighty kilometers) wide. Once known as the Black Swamp region, this area was drained by early settlers. Now the valuable agricultural land supports numerous orchards and vegetable farms. In the northeast, where the Great Lakes Plain is only five to ten miles (eight to sixteen kilometers) wide, the lake location has nurtured much of Ohio's heavy industry.

The glacier polished most of western Ohio into smooth plains highlighted by rolling hills. Called the Till Plain, this region is part of the nation's Corn Belt and boasts some of the finest farmland in the nation.

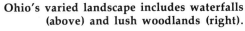
Ohio's varied landscape includes waterfalls
(above) and lush woodlands (right).

In eastern Ohio, not far from the present-day city of Akron, the last glacier came to rest and began its slow retreat. Untouched by the ice sheet, southeastern Ohio remains a land of steep, thrusting hills and winding valleys. This region, known as the Allegheny Plateau, is the westernmost part of the Appalachian Plateau, a rugged chain of mountains that stretches south to Alabama. The land of the Allegheny Plateau yields a rich supply of coal and natural gas, but the thin soil is a trial to the farmer. Today, much of the land is covered with forest.

RIVERS AND LAKES

A series of long, low hills crosses the state from the northeast corner to Marion County along the western border. North of this divide, rivers such as the Maumee, Grand, Sandusky, Portage, Vermilion, Cuyahoga, and Ashtabula flow northward to empty

The Ohio River, shown here near Cincinnati, is the most important river in the state.

into Lake Erie. Nearly all of Ohio's large rivers, however, lie south of the divide and empty into the Ohio River. Ohio's longer rivers include the Muskingum, Hocking, Tuscarawas, Great Miami, and Little Miami. The Great Miami and the Little Miami run approximately parallel to one another and form a broad, fertile valley. The longest and widest river lying entirely within the state is the Scioto.

But it is the Ohio River that is the lifeline of the state. The Ohio stretches more than 450 miles (724 kilometers) along the state's southeast and southern border. The Ohio River links Ohio—and its eastern border states—with the vast Mississippi River system and the Gulf of Mexico. The Ohio is a major artery for cargo ships and is one of the nation's most important commercial waterways. To accommodate large cargo vessels, the river channel has been dredged and deepened repeatedly so that all parts of the river are at least nine feet (three meters) deep. In addition, forty-six dams along the river's course work to raise or lower ships past points where the river rises or falls abruptly. Fortunately, despite the industrial traffic, there are still wild stretches along the Ohio where sycamores and willow thickets hug the shore.

A lighthouse on the Marblehead Peninsula along Lake Erie

Lake Erie is to northern Ohio what the Ohio River is to the south—a vital link to the wider world. Since the St. Lawrence Seaway opened in 1959, oceangoing vessels have had access to Lake Erie and to the other Great Lakes. Ohio manufacturers can now ship their goods directly by water to ports anywhere in the world.

Lake Erie's shoreline stretches along 312 miles (502 kilometers) of bluffs, beaches, and rocks from Toledo to Conneaut. Here and there, the shore is cut by bays and inlets that serve as fine natural harbors. Sandusky Bay, cradled between Cedar Point and the Marblehead Peninsula, has a 53-mile (85-kilometer) shoreline. Northwest of the bay's mouth, several loosely clustered islands have become popular summer spots. These include Kelleys Island and North, Middle, and South Bass islands.

More than twenty-five hundred lakes lie wholly within Ohio.

Ohio boasts stunning autumn foliage (left) and such beautiful wildflowers as blazing stars (above).

About twenty of the state's natural lakes cover forty acres (sixteen hectares) or more. Many Ohio lakes were created to serve as flood-control reservoirs, while others were engineered in the nineteenth century to feed water into the state's canals. Grand Lake, formed in the 1840s as part of the Miami and Erie Canal system, is the largest lake lying entirely within the state.

FLORA AND FAUNA

About one-fourth of Ohio's land area—mostly in the southern section of the state—is covered with forests. Hardwood trees such as beech, hickory, maple, sycamore, and oak are common throughout the state. The horse chestnut, or buckeye tree, gives Ohio its nickname, the Buckeye State. In the spring, buckeye trees are covered with clusters of creamy white flowers that later develop into thick-shelled nuts. The spring thaw carpets the

Wild turkeys (above) and white-tailed deer (right) are among the many animals that can be found in Ohio.

woodlands and meadows with arbutus, anemones, Indian pipes, blazing stars, and other wildflowers.

When the first white settlers reached Ohio, wolves, bears, bison, and deer roamed the region. Today, however, the white-tailed deer is the only large animal to survive in the state. Rabbits, squirrels, raccoons, opossums, skunks, woodchucks, and red foxes are still abundant. Mink and muskrats live along some lakes and streams. Ducks and other shorebirds nest along Lake Erie, and hawks and bald eagles sometimes circle in the skies. Wild turkeys were reestablished in the state during the 1950s, and are now plentiful enough to be hunted during a controlled season. The state's numerous rivers are home to game fish such as bass, bluegill, catfish, muskellunge, perch, and pike.

CLIMATE

Every fall, thousands of people flock to the town of Vermilion to hear the forecast for the coming winter at the annual Woolly Bear Festival. According to tradition, the orange and black stripes of the woolly bear caterpillar serve as weather predictors. If the orange bands are narrow, the winter will be mild, but if they are wide, blizzards and severe cold lie ahead.

In general, Ohio winters are cold, with an average January temperature of 28 degrees Fahrenheit (minus 2 degrees Celsius). Extremely cold weather is rare, but can occur. The coldest temperature ever recorded in the state was minus 39 degrees Fahrenheit (minus 39 degrees Celsius) at Milligan on February 10, 1899. While snowfall averages 29 inches (74 centimeters) a year throughout the state, the "snow belt" along Lake Erie east of Cleveland is frequently buried under blizzards in the winter. The town of Chardon, for example, receives an average of 108 inches (274 centimeters) of snow each winter.

July temperatures in Ohio average a gentle 73 degrees Fahrenheit (23 degrees Celsius), but sizzling heat waves are all too common. The state's highest temperature reading was 113 degrees Fahrenheit (45 degrees Celsius), recorded at Thurman in 1897 and at Gallipolis in 1934.

The state's average yearly precipitation (rain, snow, and other moisture) is 38 inches (97 centimeters). The driest area of the state, receiving about 32 inches (81 centimeters) of yearly precipitation, is in the north along Lake Erie. The wettest part of the state is in the southwest, where yearly precipitation averages about 44 inches (112 centimeters).

Ohio is the easternmost state in America's "tornado belt." Every spring and fall, funnel clouds whip over the countryside, snatching up trees, cars, cattle, and any unfortunate human beings in their path. In 1974, thirty-seven people died and about two thousand were injured in a series of twelve storms, one of which nearly destroyed the town of Xenia. On May 31, 1985, a tornado killed nine people in Niles and leveled one-fourth of the buildings in Newton Falls. Ohioans have learned to look out for the early warning signs of tornadoes, and to rebuild the towns and their lives in the wake of these disastrous storms.

Chapter 3
THE
PEOPLE

THE PEOPLE

Wapakoneta, New Boston, Gnadenhutten, Dublin, Zaleski. The names of these Ohio towns recall the Native Americans, New Englanders, and German, Irish, and Eastern European immigrants who helped to build Ohio. These peoples and countless others shaped the character of Ohio today.

POPULATION AND POPULATION DISTRIBUTION

With 10,797,624 people according to the 1980 census, Ohio ranks sixth among the states in population, though it is only thirty-fifth in size. Ohio averages about 261 people per square mile (101 people per square kilometer), making the state one of the ten most densely populated in the nation. About 73 percent of all Ohioans live in urban areas—cities or suburbs. The remaining 27 percent live in small towns or on farms scattered across Ohio's sprawling rural regions.

Ohio has been described as a carpet of agriculture studded by great cities. One of the most industrial states in the nation, it claims seven cities with populations exceeding 100,000. In order of size (according to the 1980 census), these cities are Cleveland, Columbus, Cincinnati, Toledo, Akron, Dayton, and Youngstown. All of Ohio's major cities, as well as many smaller communities, developed along waterways. Cleveland, Toledo, Lorain, and Sandusky began as small ports on Lake Erie. Cincinnati arose on

A participant in the annual Columbus Marathon is followed by bicyclists monitoring the race.

the banks of the Ohio; Dayton nestles in the forks of the Great Miami; Columbus (the state capital) straddles the Scioto River. Akron and a string of smaller manufacturing cities cluster along the valley of the Mahoning River.

Northeastern Ohio, where factories and refineries hug the lake and bristle along the rivers, is the most densely populated region of the state. In central and western Ohio, on the eastern fringe of America's vast Corn Belt, fields of corn and wheat and grazing land for cattle surround such large cities as Columbus and Dayton, as well as smaller cities and towns. The Allegheny Plateau in the southeast, with its coal mines and scattered farms, is almost entirely rural.

POPULATION GROWTH

Although Ohio's population grew slowly during colonial times, after statehood in 1803 its population growth was remarkable. In the first seven years of statehood, Ohio's population increased

500 percent—from 45,365 to 230,760. The population doubled during the next ten years, reaching 581,434 in 1820. This growth continued throughout the nineteenth century, and by 1850, with a population of approximately 2 million, Ohio had become the third-most-populous state in the nation. Ohio's population has continued to increase throughout the twentieth century, though at a considerably slower rate. Between 1970 and 1980, the population of the United States rose 11.45 percent. In contrast, Ohio experienced only a 1.3 percent population gain. A drastic loss of jobs in heavy industry discouraged immigration to the state, and many Ohioans left to find work in other parts of the country.

WHO ARE THE OHIOANS?

The overwhelming majority of Ohioans—97 percent—were born in the United States. Their ancestors, however, came to the Buckeye State from all over the globe. Men and women of British descent came from the older, seaboard states to establish the first permanent white settlements in Ohio. Most came in search of farmland, but some also sought religious freedom. The Shakers, a religious group noted for their exuberant dancing, established communities that flourished until the 1850s in Warren and Butler counties. In the early 1800s, Germans came to the manufacturing and farming regions of the state. Welsh settlers arrived to develop the mineral resources in southern Ohio. In the 1820s, Irish immigrants came to Ohio to work on the state's canals and railroads. The 1880s and 1890s brought a tide of newcomers from eastern and southern Europe—including Poles, Hungarians, Slovenians, Russians, and Italians—who took jobs in the factories of Ohio's mushrooming cities.

In the years before the Civil War, many blacks fled the southern

slave states and settled in Ohio. A greater period of black
migration began during World War I and continued into the early
1950s. Today, about 9 percent of Ohioans are black, and 1 percent
are Hispanic. In recent years, northeastern Ohio has experienced
an influx of immigrants from the Middle East and Asia.

RELIGION

Roman Catholics comprise the largest single religious group in
Ohio. The Lutheran, Methodist, and Presbyterian churches and
the United Church of Christ are the state's most widely followed
Protestant denominations. Cleveland, Columbus, Cincinnati, and
other Ohio cities have sizable Jewish populations. The Hebrew
Union College-Jewish Institute of Religion in Cincinnati is the
oldest Jewish theological school in the country. Moslem mosques
stand in many northeastern Ohio cities.

More Amish people live in Ohio than in any other state. In
keeping with their religious beliefs, Amish families live much as
their ancestors did, without automobiles, telephones, or electricity.
Their horse-drawn carriages can often be seen along the back
roads of Holmes and Geauga counties and on the streets of
Walnut Creek and Middlefield.

Seven United States presidents were born in Ohio: (left to right) Ulysses S. Grant, Rutherford B. Hayes, James Garfield, Benjamin Harrison, William McKinley, William Howard Taft, and Warren Harding.

POLITICS

No single political party holds sway in Ohio. Democratic support is strongest in the cities of the northeast and along the Ohio River. Republicans tend to dominate the central and western parts of the state. In the 1980s, the majority of Ohio's congressmen were Democrats, as was the state governor. In the state legislature, Democrats controlled the house of representatives, but Republicans held a majority in the senate. In general, the political views of Ohioans match those of most Americans. In a large majority of presidential elections since 1804, the winning candidate was also the winner of Ohio's electoral votes. For this reason, Ohio is sometimes referred to as a "barometer state."

Seven of America's presidents, all of them Republicans, were born in Ohio—Ulysses S. Grant, Rutherford B. Hayes, James A. Garfield, Benjamin Harrison, William McKinley, William Howard Taft, and Warren Harding. Another president, William Henry Harrison, was born in Virginia but spent much of his life in the Buckeye State. Ohio has sent more men to the White House than any other state except Virginia—earning it the nickname "Mother of Presidents."

Chapter 4

THE BEGINNING

THE BEGINNING

THE MOUND BUILDERS

People first migrated into the region we now call Ohio probably about ten thousand years ago. Most scientists believe they were the descendants of people who traveled to North America from Asia. The first Ohioans were nomads who lived by hunting game and gathering wild fruits and nuts. They eventually disappeared, leaving few traces besides their chipped flint knives and spearheads. Then, about two thousand years ago, another wave of migrants reached Ohio—the first of several groups of people commonly known as the Mound Builders.

The Ohio Valley Mound Builders, like the ancient people before them, relied primarily on hunting and fishing for their existence. They also practiced some farming. Unlike their predecessors, however, these people left behind a remarkable record of their lives. Southern Ohio is dotted with more than ten thousand earthen mounds—great hills carefully shaped by human hands. Many are round with broad, flat tops. Some are cone-shaped, and others are shaped like animals. The Great Serpent Mound near Hillsboro in Adams County resembles an immense, partially coiled snake that stretches for nearly a quarter of a mile (two-fifths of a kilometer). Clenched in the serpent's enormous jaws is an egg-shaped mound measuring thirty feet (nine meters) across.

Many of the mounds were used to mark the graves of important members of the community. One mound, excavated near Chillicothe, contained a tomb lined with weapons and ornaments

Obsidian spear points (top left), incised pottery (above), copper ornaments (far left), and stone pipes (left) are among the many artifacts that have been uncovered at Mound City Group National Monument near Chillicothe.

of beaten copper. The Mound Builders sometimes erected high earthen walls around their villages, perhaps for defense. At Fort Ancient near Lebanon, three miles (five kilometers) of walls enclose nearly one hundred acres (forty hectares) of land.

The most highly developed of these mound-building civilizations was the Hopewell Culture, named for the Hopewell farm where archaeologists first studied its remains. The Hopewell people flourished throughout the Ohio Valley from about 100 B.C. to A.D. 500. Anthropologists believe that they had developed a multilevel society that had a defined organization and code of conduct. Such a society would be needed to complete such tasks as building the great mounds. There is evidence that the Hopewell people had an extensive trade network that reached throughout the Midwest, the Mississippi Valley, and the eastern seacoast. This theory is supported by the Michigan copper, Minnesota pipestone, Rocky Mountain obsidian, and Caribbean conch shells that have been found in Hopewell tombs.

The Mound Builders vanished long before the first white explorers reached Ohio. By the early 1700s, Ohio was the home of about fifteen thousand people belonging to several Indian groups.

During this time, a powerful federation of tribes called the Iroquois Nation fanned out from present-day New York State into ever more-distant territory. In 1656, the Iroquois nearly annihilated the Eries, who once fished and hunted along the eastern shore of the lake that bears their name. The Delawares (who called themselves the Lenni Lenape), also fleeing from Iroquois domination, crossed the Allegheny Mountains from Pennsylvania into Ohio and settled in the Muskingum Valley. The Iroquois drove the Wyandots into present-day Marion, Crawford, and Wyandot counties. At the height of their power, in the early 1700s, the Iroquois controlled most of the Indian peoples living from the St. Lawrence to the Tennessee River and as far west as the Mississippi River.

In the Ohio Valley lived the wandering Shawnees, who migrated north from Kentucky and North Carolina. A large village near the mouth of the Scioto River became the seat of Shawnee power in Ohio. Eventually, the Shawnees formed a crucial alliance with the Miamis, who lived in western Ohio and in portions of present-day Indiana and Michigan.

The Indian peoples who lived in Ohio hunted and traded, waged war and made peace with one another. Then, early in the eighteenth century, they encountered an adversary who would shatter their way of life forever.

VYING FOR THE LAND

As early as 1669, French adventurer René-Robert Cavelier, Sieur de La Salle, may have set foot on Ohio soil during his exploration of the Great Lakes region. By 1673, maps drawn in Paris identified the land drained by the rivers that emptied into Lake Erie or the Ohio River as French territory. Meanwhile, the British claimed the land that stretched inland from the coastal colonies, including the land of present-day Ohio. In 1749, with great ceremony, French explorer Céloron de Bienville planted a series of engraved lead plates along the Ohio River to reiterate the French claim on the Ohio Valley. By that time, however, British fur traders were already well established in the territory and had won many Indian allies.

Long rivals in Europe, the French and the British competed fiercely for land, power, and precious beaver pelts along the Great Lakes. Their conflicts finally erupted into a series of bloody wars, known as the French and Indian Wars, in which they battled over claims in North America for nearly eighty years. The British gained the mighty Iroquois as unshakable allies, while the French enlisted the aid of many of the Iroquois's enemies.

An important battle during the French and Indian Wars occurred at Pickawillany, a Miami Indian village at the junction of Loramie Creek and the Great Miami River. The village, a cluster of some sixty cabins within stockade walls, had become a thriving trading post. For a time, both French and English fur traders made regular visits to Pickawillany. Eventually, however, the English won the support of the Miamis in their struggle with the French. The Miami chief became so loyal that he earned the nickname "Old Britain." On a June morning in 1752, when most of the Miami warriors were away on a hunting expedition, French commander Charles Langlade and a group of Indians sympathetic to the French took the post completely by surprise. They plundered the storerooms of furs and ammunition, murdered Old Britain, and burned the fort to the ground.

Moravian missionary David Zeisberger, shown here preaching to the Indians, established the mission town of Schoenbrunn in 1772.

The last of the French and Indian Wars ended in 1763, when a treaty awarded England nearly all of the French-claimed territory east of the Mississippi. With the French gone, an Ottawa chief named Pontiac organized many of the Great Lakes tribes in a concerted effort to drive the British, too, from Indian territory. Several British outposts, including the fort at Sandusky, fell under Indian assaults. The British hoped to keep peace by forbidding white settlements west of the Alleghenies. But the new rule was soon violated. More and more British and Scottish trappers, traders, and settlers crossed the mountains into Ohio.

One Delaware chief, realizing that the settlers were there to stay, invited a group of Moravian missionaries to instruct his people in the ways of the whites. The Protestant Moravians had been persecuted in their native Germany for their religious beliefs, especially for their refusal to fight in wars. The Delawares, too, were peace-loving people, and the venture was a success. On the Tuscarawas River near present-day New Philadelphia, a group of

Moravians established the mission town of Schoenbrunn in 1772. They converted many Delawares to Christianity, and taught Indian children at Ohio's first schoolhouse.

WAR AND INDEPENDENCE

In 1776, the thirteen British colonies along the Atlantic coast declared their independence from the mother country. The British hoped to hold onto the territory west of the Alleghenies by enlisting the help of many Indian groups. However, frontier General George Rogers Clark secured Ohio and much of the land stretching west to the Mississippi for the Americans.

Tension ran high among the scattered Ohio settlers. Both British and colonial sympathizers mistrusted the peace-loving Moravians and their Indian converts. In 1781, the British tried several of the missionaries as American spies. The following year, American troops captured a band of Delawares who had been taught by the Moravians. The captive Indians prayed and sang hymns through the night. In the morning, sixty-two adults and thirty-four children were executed by colonists sympathetic to the revolutionary cause.

The Revolutionary War broke the ties that bound the colonies to Great Britain. Ohio lay at the eastern edge of the vast Northwest Territory, a region now in the hands of the young American nation. In 1787, Congress drew up the Northwest Ordinance, a body of laws to govern these western lands. The Northwest Ordinance contained a provision by which sections of the territory could apply for statehood once the population reached sixty thousand. It also set aside land in every township to be used to finance public education, and outlawed slavery and involuntary servitude in the territory.

Chapter 5
THE ROAD TO STATEHOOD

THE ROAD TO STATEHOOD

TOWNS IN THE FOREST

At the Bunch of Grapes Tavern in Boston, two New Englanders helped to chart the course of Ohio's history. In early 1786, Manasseh Cutler and General Rufus Putnam, both veterans of the Revolutionary War, met at the tavern with a group of businessmen. Their goal was to form a company that would purchase lands in Ohio from the United States government and then sell these lands to New Englanders who wished to settle in the Ohio region. The Ohio Company purchased 1.5 million acres (.6 million hectares) of land in what is now southeastern Ohio from the United States government. Advertising in New England newspapers for people to help settle the territory, the company claimed, "[We] are fully satisfied that the lands in [the Ohio country] are of much better quality than any others known to New England People."

In April 1788, a clumsy riverboat called the *Adventure Gallery*, carrying forty-eight men recruited by the company, made its way down the Ohio River to anchor at the mouth of the Muskingum River. Accustomed to the harsh, stony soil of Massachusetts and Connecticut, the recruits were delighted by Ohio's rich, dark earth. Within three days, they had cleared 4 acres (1.6 hectares) of land near the thickly wooded Ohio River banks. With the logs of the felled trees they erected a sturdy fort that they named Campus Martius.

Six weeks after the men arrived, their wives and children reached the settlement and devoted themselves to the work of clearing the land and keeping house. The settlers named their village Marietta in honor of French queen Marie Antoinette. The first permanent white community in Ohio, Marietta grew into a thriving river town.

In late 1788, a flatboat loaded with families from New Jersey floated down the Ohio past the infant settlement of Marietta to the mouth of the Little Miami River. There, the newcomers established the village of Losantiville. Two years later, Arthur St. Clair arrived in the Ohio region to serve as the Northwest Territory's first governor. St. Clair was a proud member of an organization of Revolutionary War officers called the Society of the Cincinnati. He changed the name of Losantiville to Cincinnati in honor of the society.

A large tract of land along the Ohio between the Scioto River and the Great Miami was claimed by Virginia. The area was called the Virginia Military District, and parcels of the district were awarded to Virginians as payment for their service during the Revolutionary War.

Lands north of the Ohio River were also opened to settlement. Until 1800, the state of Connecticut claimed the Western Reserve, a 120-mile (193-kilometer) strip of land along Lake Erie west of the Pennsylvania border. In 1796, a group of surveyors, led by Moses Cleaveland, laid out a town at the center of the Western Reserve, where the Cuyahoga River flows into Lake Erie. Cleaveland boasted that the settlement that bore his name (though the spelling was later changed to Cleveland) would someday be as large as his hometown of Wyndham, Connecticut. At the time, Cleaveland's prediction seemed laughable. Even after a few years, the settlement on the lake had only seven permanent residents.

Marietta, established in 1788, was the first permanent white settlement in Ohio.

Lands farther west along Lake Erie, at the western edge of the reserve, were soon settled as well. These lands, called the Firelands, were awarded to Connecticut citizens whose farms and homes had been burned or destroyed by British troops during the Revolutionary War.

INDIAN OPPOSITION

The settlers at Marietta staged a gala celebration for their first Fourth of July in Ohio. Their Indian neighbors joined them for a spectacular feast of venison, turkey, pork, and fish—including an enormous pike over six feet (two meters) long.

But as white settlers encroached even deeper into Indian territory, this spirit of friendship faded away. In the winter of 1791, Indian warriors killed a band of settlers at Big Bottom on the Muskingum River and burned the settlers' half-finished blockhouse. Indian raiding parties spread terror as they ambushed

General "Mad" Anthony Wayne   Chief Little Turtle

hunters and attacked remote farms, burning cabins and killing
men, women, and children.

In 1792, Arthur St. Clair, who was military commander as well
as governor of the Northwest Territory, marched his army north
to the Maumee River to quell the Indian uprising. However, a
Miami chief named Little Turtle saw, as Pontiac had years earlier,
the value of uniting several Indian tribes. A combined force of
Miamis, Shawnees, and Delawares under Little Turtle surrounded
St. Clair at night and killed seven hundred of his men.

After this crushing defeat, St. Clair resigned as military
commander. His replacement was a fiery young general who had
earned a reputation for boldness and daring during the
Revolutionary War. "Mad" Anthony Wayne was determined to
break Indian resistance in Ohio forever. He drilled his troops
relentlessly, and recruited a band of scouts who had lived among
the Indians and knew their languages and customs. Among his
recruits was William Wells, who at age twelve had been captured

Chief Little Turtle's defeat in the Battle of Fallen Timbers (above) marked the end of Indian resistance in the Ohio region.

by the Miamis and adopted by Little Turtle. Though he previously had fought for the Indians against St. Clair and his forces, Wells now allied himself with the white invaders led by Wayne.

After a year of preparation, four disciplined divisions under General Wayne met Little Turtle and his men near present-day Defiance. A recent storm had ripped down a clump of trees, which lay in a dense tangle of trunks and branches. After an hour of brutal fighting, the outcome was clear. Little Turtle's defeat at the Battle of Fallen Timbers marked the end of Indian resistance in the Northwest Territory. In 1795, by the Treaty of Greenville, the Indians ceded their Ohio lands—nearly two-thirds of the present-day state—to the United States.

This one-room structure in Marietta, which once served as the Ohio Land Office, is the oldest office building in Ohio.

THE RUSH TO THE LAND

No longer terrorized by Indian raids, more and more white families poured across the Alleghenies into Ohio. Axes rang through the forests, and rough log cabins sprouted up in the clearings. Today, Americans sometimes romanticize life in a log cabin, but in reality it was far from glamorous. In summer, insects crept through chinks between the logs. In winter, the icy fingers of the wind found their way inside. Many settlers longed for the comforts of life in the East: open roads, cleared fields, and gatherings of neighbors. Yet when they wrote to their friends and relatives, they sent glowing descriptions of the fertile farmland, land so plentiful that there was enough for all who were willing to clear the forests. Despite the hardships, they encouraged their friends to cross the mountains to Ohio.

The oldest office building in Ohio stands in the city of Marietta. Erected in 1788, the one-room log-and-clapboard structure once served as the Ohio Land Office. In the early 1800s, immigrants from the eastern states flocked to land offices along the Ohio frontier to purchase as many acres as they could afford. To this day, people often refer to booming sales as "a land-office business."

As soon as they arrived, the settlers built churches, schools, and courthouses in an effort to re-create the towns they had left behind. Tireless ax blades bit ever deeper into the forest, yet the supply of trees and game seemed inexhaustible. There were plenty of logs for cabins, rail fences, and firewood. Animals of the forest were abundant, too. Some settlers paid for their land with wolf skins, which fetched a bounty of $4.25 apiece. The people of Amesville bought the books for their library by selling raccoon pelts.

THE SEVENTEENTH STATE

In 1800, Congress carved up the Northwest Territory. The western part of the territory became the Territory of Indiana, while the eastern part—the land of present-day Ohio—continued to be known as the Northwest Territory. Chillicothe, on the Scioto River, was chosen as the capital of the new Northwest Territory. In November 1802, a convention met at Chillicothe to draft a state constitution. On March 3, 1803, Ohio, with a population approaching seventy thousand, became the seventeenth state to enter the Union.

The state government remained at Chillicothe until 1810, when it was moved to Zanesville. Two years later, Chillicothe again became the capital. However, most Ohio officials wanted a centrally located seat of government that could be reached easily by people from every part of the state. They chose a spot north of Chillicothe near the middle of the state. In 1816, Columbus was inaugurated as Ohio's permanent state capital.

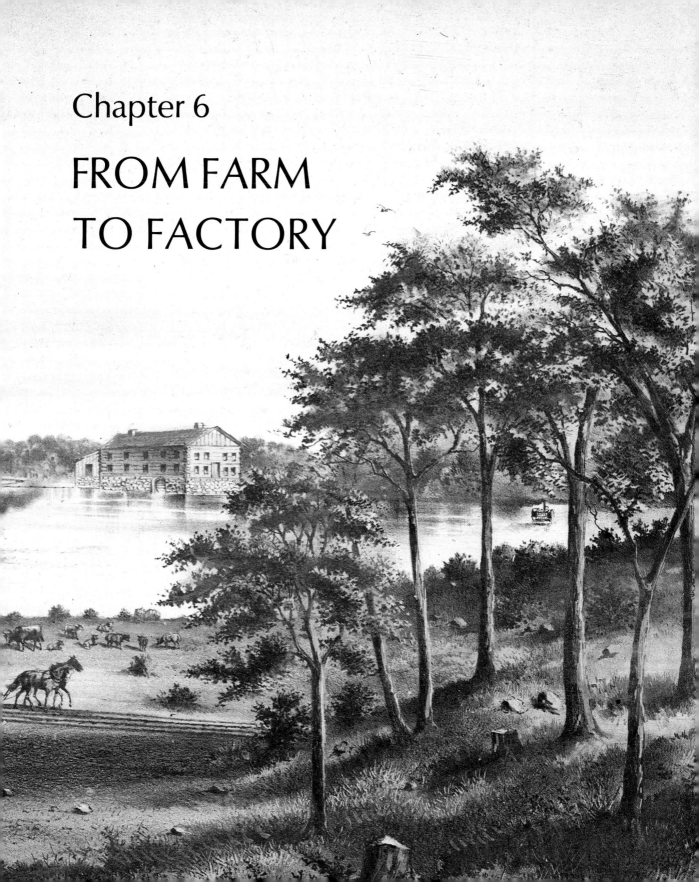

Chapter 6

FROM FARM
TO FACTORY

FROM FARM TO FACTORY

In the 1830s, French writer Alexis de Tocqueville toured the
United States. The Ohioans impressed him as "a people without
precedents, without traditions . . . cutting out their institutions like
their roads in the midst of the forest which they have come to
inhabit and where they are sure to encounter neither limits nor
obstacles. Success unlimited seems destined there."

Ohio farmers soon found that they could produce more food
than their families needed. It was difficult, however, for them to
sell their surplus, for between the Buckeye State and the eager
markets in the East rose the rugged Allegheny Mountains. Many
farmers converted bulky grain to flour or whiskey, which could
be transported more easily. They salted pork so that it would keep
on the long journey. Then they loaded their goods onto
packhorses for the wearying trek over the mountains.

RIVERBOATS

The Louisiana Purchase of 1803 opened the doors of the eastern
markets to the Ohio farmer. Goods, livestock, and produce could
be shipped down the Ohio and then the Mississippi to New
Orleans. From there, the goods could be shipped to the cities
along the East Coast. It was a longer trip than the one over the
mountains, but a much easier one.

A steamboat at Marietta Wharf in the early 1800s

The earliest riverboats were of little help to the Ohio farmer. Flatboats—large raftlike boats—traveled regularly along the Ohio River, but they could travel only one way—downstream. They were too large and clumsy to be maneuvered against the current. Long, narrow keelboats could make the round trip, but the upstream journey was laborious, requiring the crew to pole the boat against the strong current. Then, in 1811, a steam-powered vessel called the *New Orleans* chugged out of Pittsburgh. The boat had two masts with sails, a tall chimney, and two enormous wheels churning at its sides. The *New Orleans* was the first steamboat to puff its way down the Ohio and Mississippi rivers. Best of all, its steam power allowed it to travel up the Mississippi and Ohio rivers as well. Soon, steamboats became Ohio's lifeline, and a new culture grew up around them.

For wealthy passengers, steamboat travel offered every conceivable luxury. In the dining room they could linger over a five-course meal to the accompaniment of a small orchestra. Staterooms had inlaid woodwork, plush carpets, and oil paintings on the walls. Livestock and cargo, as well as passengers who could not afford expensive fares, were crowded into the lower decks. These less fortunate passengers slept on piles of boxes and drank the foul water of the river. Steamboat travel could be dangerous as well as uncomfortable. Overworked boilers sometimes exploded, causing disastrous fires. By the 1840s, as many as one hundred boats a year burned and sank.

CANALS AND RAILROADS

Farmers in central Ohio, away from the Ohio River or Lake Erie, needed more than steamboats to ship their goods. The rivers and creeks in central Ohio were often not large enough or deep enough for steamboat travel. The farmers needed a way to get their goods from the farms to the waterways plied by the steamboats. In 1823, a Cleveland lawyer named Alfred Kelley drafted a plan for a statewide system of canals. In 1825, he became Ohio's canal commissioner, overseeing the vast project he had designed. He visited the excavation sites, ate with the workmen, and somehow managed to keep the cost within the state's budget.

The project included the building of two major canals. The Ohio and Erie Canal, completed in 1832, ran the length of the state from Portsmouth on the Ohio River to Cleveland on Lake Erie. The Miami and Erie Canal, completed in 1845, stretched from the southern city of Cincinnati to Toledo. Teams of mules plodded the towpath on the canal banks, hauling the boats slowly but steadily along. One mule driver who worked on the Ohio and Erie Canal

Tour guides at the Piqua Historical Area demonstrate how, in the 1800s, canal boats were pulled along the Miami and Erie Canal by mules who plodded along its banks.

was a young man named James A. Garfield. Years later, when he became president of the United States, he recalled that during his six weeks on the job, he fell into the canal fourteen times.

The Ohio and Erie Canal was scarcely completed when railroads came to Ohio. The state's first railroad, the Erie and Kalamazoo, was completed in 1836. The abundance of lumber, the arrival of immigrant workers, and the needs of the Ohio economy spurred railroad development. By 1860, railroads connected Ohio cities with several major Atlantic coastal cities, and Ohio earned the nickname "Gateway to the West." Indeed, the railroads proved so effective that the canals soon fell into disuse.

CHANGING OHIO

First the steamboats and then the canals and railroads brought prosperity to Ohio. Land prices soared. By the 1840s, Ohio led the nation in the production of wheat, corn, and wool. The population of Cleveland doubled and then doubled again, far outstripping Moses Cleaveland's hometown of Wyndham,

Cincinnati as it appeared in 1845

Connecticut. Cincinnati became the pork and sausage capital of the world and was nicknamed "Porkopolis." In 1848, Horace Greeley, editor of the *New York Tribune*, predicted that in fifty years, Cincinnati would be the greatest city on earth. By 1850, Ohio had become the third-most-populous state in the nation.

The ethnic makeup of Ohio was also changing. Irish workmen came to dig canals and stayed on to work in the growing cities. Thousands of Germans found jobs in Cincinnati's slaughterhouses and packing plants. Yet, despite its new cosmopolitan flavor, Ohio clung to its reputation as a frontier state.

In 1840, a Virginia-born Ohioan named William Henry Harrison ran for the office of president of the United States. As a United States Army general, Harrison had led his troops to victory against the Indians in the Battle of Tippecanoe, Indiana, in 1811. During his presidential campaign, one opposing editorial argued that "the general is better fitted to sit in a log cabin and drink hard cider than to rule in the White House." Harrison's

This song was composed to emphasize the ''log-cabin'' theme of William Henry Harrison's 1840 presidential campaign.

supporters took up the challenge. They built miniature cabins of buckeye logs and set them on wagons to campaign for Harrison throughout the state. William Henry Harrison became the nation's first ''log-cabin'' president.

INTO CIVIL WAR

> Eliza made her desperate retreat across the river just in the dusk of twilight. The gray mist of evening, rising slowly from the river, enveloped her as she disappeared up the bank, and the swollen current and floundering masses of ice presented a hopeless barrier to her pursuer.

The slave woman Eliza's flight to freedom across the ice-choked Ohio River is one of the most gripping scenes in Harriet Beecher Stowe's 1852 novel *Uncle Tom's Cabin*. Written while the author lived in Cincinnati, the book triggered waves of antislavery sentiment across the nation.

During the 1840s and 1850s, debates over the slavery issue wracked the country. Ohio's 1803 constitution prohibited slavery within the state. Most people in northern Ohio agreed that slavery was one of the greatest evils human beings could inflict on one another. At the same time, many people in southern Ohio, the descendants of Virginians, sympathized with the South. As the slavery question tore the country further and further apart, Ohio, too, felt the rising tension.

Hundreds of runaway slaves, like Eliza, escaped from Kentucky and Virginia into Ohio. They slipped across the state from one "safe house" to another, traveling by a secret system known as the Underground Railroad. Sympathetic farmers transported slaves in wagons beneath loads of wheat or hay. Families hid them in barns, cellars, and attics. When the runaways reached Lake Erie, they boarded boats to Canada, where no slave hunters could pursue them.

In September 1858, slave hunters captured an eighteen-year-old boy named John Price in the small college town of Oberlin. They planned to return him to his owner in Kentucky and collect a reward. Within hours, hundreds of men thundered out of Oberlin in pursuit. At Wellington, they stormed the hotel where the slave hunters were spending the night, rescued John Price, and helped him escape to Canada. Charged with having violated federal fugitive slave laws, thirty-seven of the men were arrested for taking part in the Oberlin-Wellington Rescue. Letters of support poured in from all over the northern states. In Cleveland, businesses shut their doors during the trial, and ten thousand people held a protest meeting in the Public Square. The audience in the courtroom cheered when Charles Langston, a free black

In the mid-1800s, abolitionists in Ohio helped runaway slaves escape to freedom along the secret system known as the Underground Railroad.

man who had participated in the rescue, declared, "When I come to be claimed by some perjured wretch as his slave, I shall never be taken into slavery. I stand here to say that I will do all I can for any man seized and held." Only two of the prisoners were found guilty, and even these charges were finally dropped.

After cannons roared at Fort Sumter, South Carolina, in 1861, President Abraham Lincoln called for Union troops to fight the newly formed Confederate States of America. Some thirty thousand Ohioans volunteered. In the summer of 1861, Ohio troops under General George McClellan drove the Confederate army out of western Virginia and secured that region for the Union.

However, as the war dragged on and grim news reached Ohio from southern battlefields, morale began to sag. A new group

This 1863 political cartoon portrays the Union being threatened by the Copperheads, a political party made up of northerners who sympathized with the South.

known as the Peace Democrats (or Copperheads), who defended states' rights and opposed the Civil War, found many followers in the Buckeye State. One powerful Copperhead leader was Dayton Congressman Clement L. Vallandigham, who opposed President Lincoln and openly predicted a Confederate victory. He spoke to the worst fears of Ohio Unionists when he declared, "defeat, death, taxation . . . these are your trophies."

Early in 1863, Lincoln banished Vallandigham from Union soil. But Vallandigham would not be silenced. From Windsor, Ontario, he campaigned for the office of governor of Ohio. Though he received nearly two hundred thousand votes, Vallandigham was defeated by Unionist Republican John Brough. At the news, Lincoln sent Brough a joyful telegram: "Glory to God in the highest! Ohio has saved the nation!"

In the summer of 1863, the fighting reached Ohio itself. With an army of two thousand men, Confederate General John Hunt Morgan crossed the Ohio River into Indiana and marched toward Cincinnati. Just north of Cincinnati, Morgan attacked Fort Dennison and burned a government corral, but Union troops drove him back from the city itself. At last, his army hopelessly divided, Morgan was captured at Salineville in Columbiana County. Today, many Ohio farmhouses bear the marks of rifle balls, said to be the legacy of Morgan and his raiders.

By war's end in 1865, 340,000 Ohioans had served in the Union forces, many with remarkably distinguished records. Generals William T. Sherman, Philip Sheridan, and Ulysses S. Grant (who later became president) were all Ohioans. The state's youngest war hero was Johnny Clem, or "Johnny Shiloh," of Newark. In 1861, at the age of nine, Johnny ran off while on his way to Sunday school and joined the Union army as a drummer boy. At the bloody Battle of Shiloh, his unshakable courage inspired the men who marched to his steady beat.

THE RISE OF INDUSTRY

With its spires, columns, and arched windows, the newly completed Cincinnati Music Hall and Exposition Building was the pride of the city. In the fall of 1870, three hundred thousand people from all over the world flocked to the Exposition Hall to view 7 acres (2.8 hectares) of lavish displays on manufacturing and the fine arts.

The same year, an ambitious young businessman named John D. Rockefeller founded a new company in Cleveland. Rockefeller's Standard Oil Company, which would become one of the world's largest companies, refined Pennsylvania crude oil into kerosene to be shipped to East Coast markets and around the world.

By the end of the nineteenth century, Ohio had shifted from an agricultural economy to one based on manufacturing. Sawmills, coal docks, and blast furnaces bristled along the shores of Lake Erie and on the banks of the Cuyahoga River. Huge boats loaded with iron ore from Upper Michigan steamed into harbors at Cleveland, Lorain, and Sandusky. Youngstown sprouted the smokestacks of steel mills, and Akron became the capital of the developing rubber industry. One observer wrote in the *Atlantic Monthly* that the people of northeastern Ohio "endure [the smoke and noise] with a smile. Smoke means business, business means money, and money is the principal thing." Cities in other parts of Ohio were home to industrial titans as well. Dayton nurtured the largest manufacturer of cash registers. Toledo companies excelled in glass-related products. Columbus became a leading manufacturer of buggies. Proctor & Gamble, a Cincinnati soap manufacturer, was destined to become the world's largest producer of household products.

LABOR VERSUS MANAGEMENT

While company owners and investors made vast fortunes, thousands of laborers from Italy, Poland, Hungary, and other European nations toiled ten and twelve hours a day. Sometimes earning as little as five dollars a week, they lived in dingy, overcrowded housing in the poorest sections of the cities. In his biting essay "Oh, I'll Say We've Done Well," writer Sherwood Anderson spoke of the human costs of this sweeping industrial growth: "We Ohio men have taken as lovely a land as ever lay outdoors and have in our towns and cities put the old stamp of ourselves on it for keeps. . . . [The factory owners] did so well that a workman could get up in the morning, go through a sooty street

Members of the first executive council of the American Federation of Labor

to a factory where all he had to do all day was drill holes in a metal frame.... At night he could go home, thanking God as he walked past the finest cinder piles and trash dumps anywhere.''

Since the early 1800s, workers in Ohio had been organizing to aid each other both on and off the job. The Dayton Mechanics Society, founded in 1813, was Ohio's first official trade union. In December 1886, representatives from twenty-five unions across the country met in Columbus. There they formed the American Federation of Labor (AFL), and named labor activist Samuel Gompers as its first president. In 1890, the AFL spearheaded a nationwide strike to demand the eight-hour workday. The strike had only limited success, and the struggle between labor and management continued into the twentieth century. Today, the AFL is allied with the Congress of Industrial Organizations (CIO) and is a formidable political force.

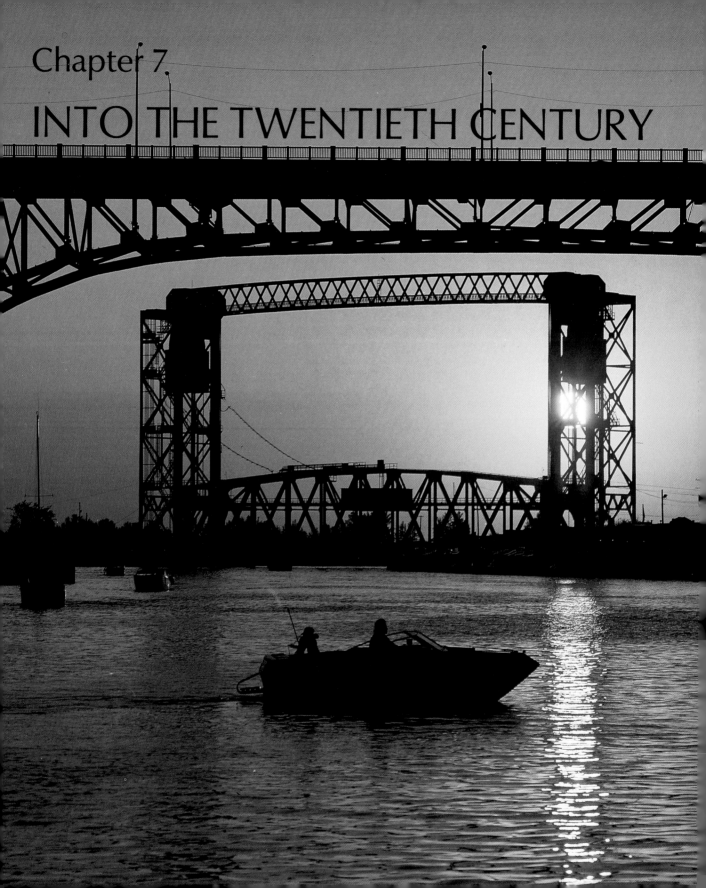

INTO THE TWENTIETH CENTURY

Reform in city government, better conditions for laborers, a vast flood-control system—Ohio saw these improvements and many others in the twentieth century. Such changes did not come, however, without a bitter struggle.

BOSSES AND REFORMERS

Mark Hanna was a wealthy businessman who owned several coal, iron, and streetcar companies. Hanna expanded his influence in the 1890s, when he entered politics and became a key leader of the Republican party. In 1896, he threw himself into the presidential campaign of Ohio's governor, William McKinley. Convinced that McKinley would promote the interests of big business, Hanna gathered contributions from industrialists across the country and launched the most expensive political campaign the nation had ever seen. McKinley's victory was assured.

Political cartoonists pictured Hanna as an organ-grinder, and McKinley his monkey on a leash. However, McKinley acted independently as president, bringing his quiet dignity to the office until he was assassinated in 1901.

While Hanna wielded his power in Cleveland, a boss of a different kind emerged in Cincinnati.

"Mr. Cox," asked journalist Lincoln Steffens, "I understand you are the boss of Cincinnati. Are you?"

"I am," George B. Cox replied.

This political cartoon shows Mark Hanna, who used his influence to help William McKinley win the 1896 presidential election, "dividing the spoils" of the presidency with McKinley.

THANKSGIVING.

"Of course, you have a mayor, a council, and judges?" Steffens continued.

"I have," said Cox. He pointed to his desk. "But I have a telephone, too."

Cincinnati tavern keeper George B. Cox entered city politics in 1884, anxious to secure protection for his business. Adept at gathering votes for friends and handing out jobs to supporters, Cox became a political power broker who controlled Cincinnati for twenty-five years. He created offices for himself and his henchmen, slashed school budgets, and handed out generous contracts for street repairs to contractors who never showed up for work. "The city is all one great graft," Steffens wrote. "Cox's system is the most perfect thing of its kind in the country, and he is proud of it."

Influence of another kind brought reform to Ohio. Tom Loftin Johnson was, like Mark Hanna, a wealthy industrialist with

In 1913, a terrible flood devastated the city of Dayton.

political ambitions. In 1901, Johnson was elected mayor of Cleveland. He approached the office with a reformer's zeal. Under his direction, parks and playgrounds were built and hundreds of miles of streets were paved. Grim poorhouses were replaced by farm colonies in the country. Johnson also championed an innovative rehabilitation program for prisoners. Cleveland's crime rate plunged, and Lincoln Steffens called it "the best-governed city in the United States."

Another mayor with radical ideas was Toledo's Sam "Golden Rule" Jones, first elected in 1897. An idealist who shared his salary with the city's poor, Jones built new schools, opened kindergartens, cleaned the streets, and put the unemployed to work.

GOOD TIMES AND BAD

The rain began on Easter Sunday, 1913. By the next day, the Miami River was a raging torrent, overflowing its banks to rampage through the streets of downtown Dayton. People huddled in attics or clung to rafts of floating debris when their homes collapsed. The flood destroyed more than $250 million in property and killed 430 people in the Miami Valley.

Spurred to action by the disaster, Ohioans raised $40 million to launch the vast Miami River Valley flood-control project. Completed in 1922, the Miami project tamed the river with five dams, sixty miles (ninety-seven kilometers) of levees, and two hundred floodgates. It was the first such project to address the entire river system rather than only the local stretch of the river.

When the United States entered World War I, Camp Sherman was hastily erected at Chillicothe to train recruits. Some 245,000 Ohioans served during the war, and 7,000 of them lost their lives. Youngstown and Cleveland supplied steel, Dayton built planes, trucks rolled from Lima assembly plants, and Akron factories churned out tires for planes and trucks. Thousands of men and women, both black and white, left the rural South to seek jobs in Ohio's war plants.

This migration continued through the 1920s, for Ohio industry boomed even after the war was over. An insatiable demand for steel was created by America's love for the automobile. Steel mills flourished in Cleveland and along the Mahoning Valley. Ohio led the nation in truck manufacturing, and only Michigan exceeded Ohio in automobile manufacturing. Construction companies pounded together houses and office buildings throughout the state. Ohio and the nation enjoyed the benefits of prosperity.

In 1929, stock prices crashed in New York, and the bubble burst. The smoky skies cleared above Cleveland, Akron, Youngstown, and Toledo as factories closed their doors. By 1933, nearly half of Ohio's workers were without jobs. In Toledo, unemployment climbed to a staggering 80 percent.

As some plants shut down and others slashed wages, labor unions began to act. When the Goodyear Tire Company planned

Striking steel workers displaying protest signs during the 1937
Youngstown Steel Strike

to cut its work force in 1936, fifteen thousand workers walked off
the job. The final settlement allowed most of the workers to keep
their jobs, but they had to agree to work only twenty-four hours a
week. In 1937, fifty thousand workers struck at seven steel plants
in Youngstown. During the weeks of unrest, five strikers were
killed and more than three hundred were wounded.

Programs under President Franklin D. Roosevelt's New Deal
put thousands of Ohioans back to work during the Great
Depression. Federal funds paid people to build roads, schools,
housing projects, and airports. Perhaps the most spectacular New
Deal project in Ohio was the Muskingum Watershed Conservancy
District, created between 1934 and 1938. The Conservancy District
covered about 20 percent of east-central Ohio, from Marietta
north to Canton and Mansfield. Throughout this region, workers
built dams and replanted forests to help control flooding and
erosion.

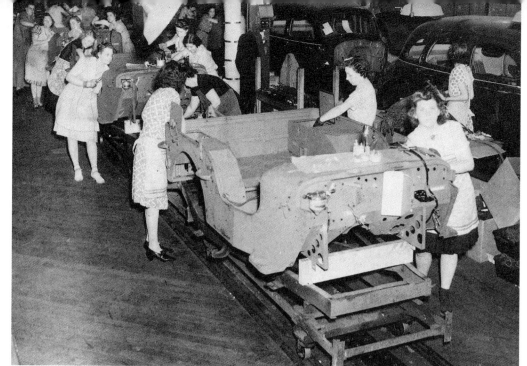

Workers on a jeep assembly line in Toledo during World War II

In 1941, the United States went to war again. Suddenly factories shouted for workers, and machinery whirred around the clock. Once again, Ohio produced steel and tires for the war effort, as well as ships, aircraft, and weapons. And once more, thousands of Ohioans put on military uniforms. Many of them never saw their homes again.

POSTWAR OHIO

Ohio prospered through the 1950s and early 1960s. The federal government was a factor in this prosperity. The National Aeronautics and Space Administration (NASA) built several large facilities in the state. Aided with federal money, the Ohio Turnpike was completed in 1955. The opening of the St. Lawrence Seaway in 1959 brought increased shipping traffic to Cleveland, Sandusky, Toledo, and other ports along Lake Erie. The seaway allowed Ohio to establish international trade and become fourth among the states in the value of goods exported.

The state's economy depended largely on heavy industries such as steel and automobile manufacturing—industries that most people thought would thrive forever.

But by the late 1960s, many plants in the Midwest began to move to the southern states, where fuel and labor were cheaper. In addition, America faced growing competition from manufacturers abroad. As more and more Ohio factories closed, unemployment rose.

VIOLENCE AT HOME

Hardest hit by the loss of jobs in heavy industry were the people living in Ohio's inner cities. Blacks were particularly vulnerable. Many had attended poorly equipped, understaffed schools and had no marketable skills. In 1966, Cleveland's predominantly black Hough district exploded in a series of riots that left whole blocks in charred ruins.

During the 1960s, black people across the nation struggled to gain their full civil rights as American citizens. In Ohio, blacks demanded a greater voice in government. In 1967, a Cleveland lawyer named Carl Stokes became the first black mayor of a major American city. His brother, Louis Stokes, was elected to the House of Representatives from Ohio's Twenty-first Congressional District. Other blacks who rose to prominence in the state during this era included William E. Walker, appointed to the governor's cabinet; and State Supreme Court Justice Robert Duncan.

Promoting Ohio as the state with the lowest taxes in the nation, Governor James Rhodes lured some new businesses that brought additional jobs to the state. Nevertheless, the overall number of jobs in the state continued to dwindle. Money became scarce; some public schools closed for lack of funds. Although Ohio

In 1970, four students were killed when National Guardsmen fired into a crowd of unarmed antiwar demonstrators at Kent State University.

needed better social services and stronger environmental protection, the state had no revenue for these increasingly pressing needs. Still, Governor Rhodes vowed never to raise state taxes.

Governor Rhodes opposed student demonstrators as firmly as he opposed increased taxation. In May 1970, he told reporters that students who protested the nation's involvement in the Vietnam conflict were "the worst kind of people we harbor in America." The next day, Rhodes called in the National Guard to control antiwar demonstrations on the campus of Kent State University. On May 4, National Guardsmen fired into a crowd of unarmed protestors, killing four student demonstrators.

CHALLENGES FOR THE FUTURE

In 1971, John J. Gilligan, a former literature professor, was elected governor and enacted Ohio's first state income tax. Gilligan used the new revenue to improve schools and human services, and to reclaim strip-mined land in the southern coal region. Although James Rhodes was reelected in 1974, income taxes in Ohio had come to stay.

In the 1970s and 1980s, the character of Ohio's cities changed dramatically. As more and more people moved to suburban areas, the populations of the major cities declined and urban areas quickly decayed. In an effort to revive their downtown sections, cities such as Cleveland, Toledo, Akron, and Cincinnati invested millions of dollars in renovations—creating convention centers, shopping malls, and parks. Though the urban poor still battle for greater opportunities in education and employment, Ohio's cities turn a hopeful face toward the future.

The condition of Ohio's lakes and rivers became a key environmental issue during the 1970s and 1980s. For generations, factories and refineries had dumped tons of pollutants into Lake Erie and Ohio's northern rivers and streams. In 1969, the nation was astounded when the heavy oil slick on the Cuyahoga River caught fire and blazed out of control. A federal report declared: "The lower Cuyahoga has no visible life, not even lower forms such as leeches and sludge worms that usually thrive on waste."

In 1972, the United States and Canada agreed to work together to clean up Lake Erie and the other Great Lakes by tightening controls on waste disposal. Though pollution remained a serious problem, Lake Erie and the rivers that feed it began to clear within a few years. To the delight of scientists and fishermen, pike and bass returned to the lake that, a decade earlier, had sustained almost no life. One biologist, Daniel White, was thrilled to discover schools of freshwater shrimp in the lake near Ashtabula, and tiny minnows called channel darters in Lorain Harbor. Describing his discoveries, White stated, "It is a sign we are to be given a second chance."

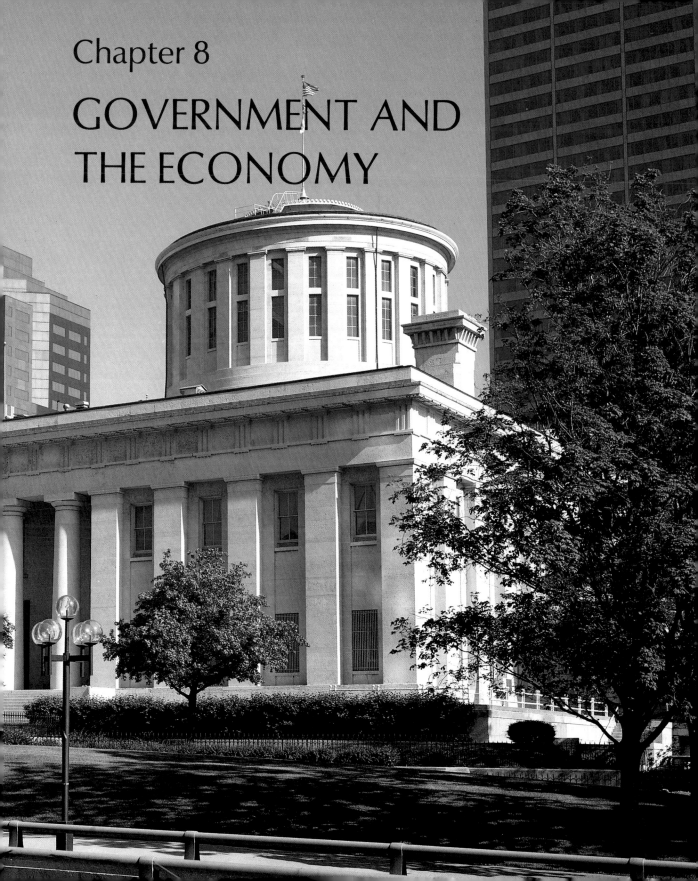

Chapter 8

GOVERNMENT AND THE ECONOMY

GOVERNMENT AND THE ECONOMY

Each year, the people of Ohio send millions of tax dollars to the state government. In return, the government provides an array of services, including education, social-welfare services, and transportation. Furthermore, the government may impose or block legislation that directly affects business in the state. Government in Ohio—as in other states—often must respond to the political and economic push and pull of special-interest groups.

GOVERNMENT

Like the federal government, Ohio's state government is divided into three main branches. The legislative branch enacts and repeals laws. The judicial branch interprets these laws, and the executive branch ensures that the laws are enforced.

Sessions of Ohio's state legislature, the General Assembly, begin on the first Monday in January in odd-numbered years. Legislative sessions have no time limit. Like the United States Congress, the General Assembly has two houses. The state senate has thirty-three members who are elected to four-year terms. The state house of representatives has ninety-nine members elected to terms of two years.

The court system in Ohio resembles a great pyramid. At the base of the pyramid are the many municipal courts in cities and towns. Each of the state's eighty-eight counties has a court of common pleas. Cases may be referred from these local courts up to one of twelve courts of appeals. At the top of the pyramid is the supreme court in Columbus, the highest court in the state. Its chief justice and six associate justices are elected to six-year terms.

Ohio's chief executive, the governor, may serve no more than two consecutive terms, although he or she can be reelected an unlimited number of times. The governor appoints the heads of many state departments, as well as the trustees of state-run universities, hospitals, and other institutions. The lieutenant governor, secretary of state, attorney general, and state treasurer are all elected officials who work within the executive branch.

REVENUE

About one-third of Ohio's revenue is generated by a personal income tax. Another third comes from taxes on retail sales, including taxes on cigarettes, gasoline, and liquor sold in state stores. Ohio also produces revenue through taxes on corporate income, inheritance, and highway use, as well as through a state lottery. Federal grants and programs provide the remainder of Ohio's revenue.

The state's revenue is dependent to a large extent on manufacturing, the most important economic activity in Ohio. When economic conditions are poor, manufacturers may decide to close factories or lay off workers. This immediately reduces the amount of revenue the state receives from the personal income tax. It also lowers the state's revenue from taxes on retail sales. This loss of revenue usually means that the state must limit the money it spends, and education, social services, industrial development, and transportation programs may suffer.

The University
of Cincinnati

EDUCATION

"Schools and the means of education shall forever be
encouraged," declared the Northwest Ordinance in 1787. Since
the earliest territorial days, Ohioans have made education a
priority. Settlers in Balpre and Marietta built one-room
schoolhouses in 1792, each family pitching in to pay the teacher's
salary. Ohio's first public schools opened in 1825. Today, all
children between the ages of six and seventeen are required to
attend school.

Ohio is the home of many outstanding colleges and universities.
Publicly funded universities include Cleveland State University;
Kent State University; Bowling Green State University; Miami
University, in Oxford; Wright State University, in Dayton; the
University of Akron; and Ohio University, in Athens. With more
than fifty thousand students at its Columbus campus, Ohio State
University boasts the largest student body of any American

Gray Chapel at Ohio Wesleyan University in Delaware

university. The University of Cincinnati, with thirty-four thousand students, is also a major academic center.

Case Western Reserve University in Cleveland, created in 1967 when Western Reserve University merged with the Case Institute of Technology, is Ohio's largest privately endowed university. It is noted for its outstanding schools of medicine and law.

Founded in 1797 as the Muskingum Academy, Marietta College in Marietta is the state's oldest institution of higher learning. Other important small colleges include Kenyon College, in Gambier; Denison University; and Ohio Wesleyan University, in Delaware. In 1920, Antioch College at Yellow Springs pioneered a unique program that allows students to alternate a semester of study with a semester of paid work. Oberlin College, founded at Oberlin in 1833, was the first coeducational college in the country, and one of the first to admit blacks. By today's standards, the first Oberlin coeds were hardly liberated. In addition to their studies, they were expected to clean the rooms of the male students and to wash and mend their clothes. Wilberforce University, founded in 1856 by the Methodist Episcopal Church, is the nation's oldest predominantly black private university. Nearby is Central State University, a predominantly black state-supported college.

Right: Supplies being transported along the Cuyahoga River Canal to Cleveland's steel-mill area
Below: Steel coils awaiting transport at the Cleveland Port Authority

TRANSPORTATION

Cars and trucks speed to every city and town in Ohio over some 112,000 miles (180,242 kilometers) of roads. The Ohio Turnpike is an east-west route across the northern part of the state. Interstate 70 offers a scenic view of central Ohio. A portion of U.S. 40 stretching from Wheeling, West Virginia, to Zanesville follows the course of the old National Road, once heavily traveled by pioneers journeying west.

Railroads have declined in importance in recent years, but ten Ohio cities are still served by passenger lines. Four freight lines still haul coal, farm produce, and other goods over 6,600 miles (10,622 kilometers) of track.

The Great Lakes and the Ohio River maintain Ohio's position as a major shipping center. Cleveland receives more iron ore than

Ohio's manufactured products are sometimes transported by railroad.

any other port in the nation. Much of it is shipped to ports on the Atlantic via the St. Lawrence Seaway. Toledo is a leading shipping center for coal. Immense tows of twenty barges or more push their way into Cincinnati to take on coal, iron ore, steel, and a host of other products bound for the Gulf of Mexico.

About twenty airlines serve Ohio's 775 airfields. The state also has two seaplane anchorages: in Lake Erie and on the Ohio River. The busiest airport in the state is Cleveland's Hopkins International Airport, followed by the airport at Columbus. The greater Cincinnati Airport is actually located across the Ohio River in Covington, Kentucky.

COMMUNICATION

Ohio's first newspaper, the *Centinel of the North-Western Territory*, appeared in Cincinnati in 1793. The *Centinel* offered information-starved frontier families five pages of three-month-old news stories and excerpts from popular novels. Today, Ohio has nearly four hundred newspapers, about a hundred of which are dailies. Leading papers in the state include the *Plain Dealer* of Cleveland, the *Cincinnati Enquirer*, the *Columbus Dispatch*, the *Blade* of Toledo, and the *Akron Beacon Journal*.

Cleveland's steel-mill area

Ohio has about 285 AM and FM radio stations. In 1922, the first radio stations in the state went on the air—WHK in Cleveland, and WOSU in Columbus. Operated by Ohio State University, WOSU was the first educational radio station in North America.

WEWS-TV, Ohio's first television station, began broadcasting in Cleveland in 1947. Today, Ohio has about fifty television stations.

GOODS AND SERVICES

Ohio's economy is based on the production of goods through manufacturing, mining, and agriculture, and on services that are sold to groups or individuals.

Manufacturing accounts for about one-third of Ohio's gross state product, or GSP, and employs 25 percent of the state's workers. (The GSP is the total value of goods and services produced in the state in a year.) Vehicles and vehicle parts are Ohio's foremost manufactured products. The state produces one-fourth of the nation's trucks. Automobiles, trucks, buses, and motorcycles are produced in Cleveland, Hudson, Lorain, Toledo,

As one of the leading industrial states in the nation, Ohio produces a large variety of manufactured products, including bricks (above).

Columbus, Cincinnati, and Springfield. Aircraft and airplane parts are manufactured in Akron, Cleveland, and Dayton. Dayton is also the headquarters of the National Cash Register Corporation, the world's largest producer of cash registers. Ohio factories also assemble farm machinery, office equipment, blast furnaces, heating and cooling equipment, and refrigeration machinery. Other goods manufactured in Ohio, in order of economic importance, include nonelectrical machinery, construction equipment, fabricated metal products, and electrical machinery. The state leads the nation in the production of household appliances.

Exceeded only by Indiana, Ohio is the nation's second-largest producer of iron and steel. About one-sixth of the country's total steel output comes from Ohio mills, chiefly those in Cleveland, Lorain, and Middletown. Ohio is also a leader in aluminum production.

Retail trade is an important aspect of Ohio's economy.

Although many of Akron's rubber factories have closed, the city still manufactures rubber products that range from conveyor belts to elastic bands. Ohio's chemical industry produces plastics, paints, and varnishes. East Liverpool and other towns along the Ohio River are known for the manufacture of bricks, tiles, and ceramic dinnerware. Cincinnati is the world's leading producer of soap and playing cards.

Food products are also important in Ohio. Cincinnati still has large meat-packing facilities. Tuscarawas County is a leader in Swiss cheese production, and all of the world's Liederkranz cheese comes from Van Wert County.

Although manufacturing is central to Ohio's economic health, service industries account for the largest portion—61 percent—of the state's GSP and employ 68 percent of the work force. The service industries include wholesale and retail trade, which together account for 16 percent of the GSP. Community, social, and personal services and government are also important service industries in Ohio.

The state's service industries are concentrated in Ohio's sixteen metropolitan areas. Columbus is a leading distribution center for department-store goods; Cleveland is a leader in wholesale trade of iron ore, machinery, and steel. Toledo trades coal and

Strip mining is the method most often used to extract Ohio's vast reserves of bituminous coal.

petroleum; Cincinnati trades coal. Cleveland is a center for private health care. Columbus is home to the finance and real-estate industries, as well as the Battelle Memorial Institute, center of the world's largest nonprofit research laboratories.

MINING

Mining accounts for about 3 percent of Ohio's GSP. Coal is the state's most valuable mineral resource. Rich beds of soft, or bituminous, coal lie beneath the land of southern Ohio, especially in Harrison and Belmont counties. Most of Ohio's coal is taken through strip mining, a process that exposes the coal by stripping away layers of earth. Strip mining has left ugly scars on the landscape, but Ohio has launched some innovative programs to reclaim damaged areas.

Ohio is a leading producer of rock salt, with numerous mines scattered through the northeast. Ohio's salt reserves could furnish the nation with all the salt it needs for the next thousand years. Quarries in Ohio yield clay for bricks and tiles, limestone and sand for glassmaking, and sandstone for building construction. About one-third of the building sandstone used in the United States comes from Ohio.

Field crops, including wheat (above), account for most of Ohio's agricultural income.

Oil drilling in Ohio began in Hancock County in the 1890s. In 1891, the McMurray Well near Van Buren was the biggest oil producer in the world. Today, however, Ohio's oil industry is relatively small.

AGRICULTURE

Ohio agriculture today employs 3 percent of the state's work force and accounts for only 2 percent of the GSP. Nevertheless, Ohio has not forgotten its heritage as a major producer of corn and wheat. Some 15.4 million acres (6.2 million hectares) of land remain under cultivation. About 272,000 people work the land on Ohio's 87,000 farms.

Corn, Ohio's staple crop since the nineteenth century, is grown throughout the state. Ohio is considered part of the nation's Corn

A pumpkin field near Toledo

Belt. The state is also a leader in the production of wheat, oats, and soybeans. Other important crops include alfalfa, barley, rye, and mushrooms.

Ohio's offshore islands and the sandy lowlands along Lake Erie are renowned for their orchards and vineyards. Ohio growers produce apples, peaches, and some of the nation's finest wine grapes. The state is also noted for its nurseries and extensive greenhouses. Ohio's hothouses help satisfy the nation's cravings for fresh vegetables through the long winter months.

Ohio farmers raise beef and dairy cattle, hogs, sheep, and poultry. A monument to the Poland China hog, a breed developed in the Miami Valley, stands near the town of Monroe. Fayette County is a center for the raising of standard-bred horses used in harness racing. Ohio produces more of these horses than does any other state. Ohio's farms, as well as its manufacturing centers, make the state a vital part of the nation's economy.

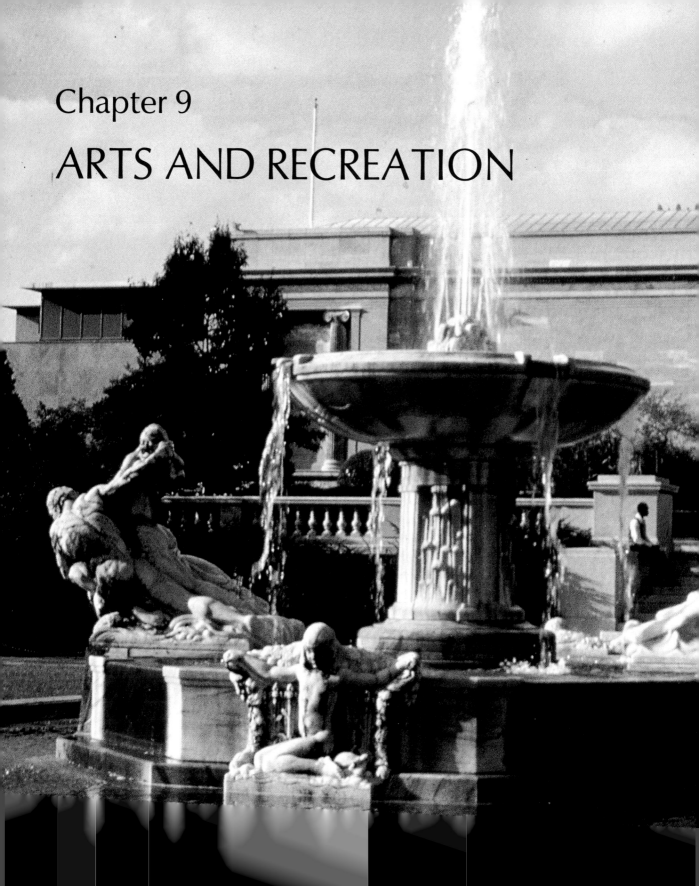

Chapter 9

ARTS AND RECREATION

ARTS AND RECREATION

One of the best ways to appreciate the character of Ohio is through noting the achievements of its people. In literature, art, music, and athletics, Ohioans have made enduring contributions that enrich the state's and the nation's heritage.

LITERATURE

In 1796, Cincinnati printer William Maxwell published a book containing the laws of the Northwest Territory. *Maxwell's Code*, as it was called, is generally considered the first book to emerge from Ohio.

The versatile Dr. Daniel Drake, sometimes called "Ohio's Ben Franklin," worked tirelessly for the advancement of education, culture, and the sciences in his city, Cincinnati. His *Picture of Cincinnati*, published in 1815, is a fascinating portrait of the town that rose on the banks of the Ohio River.

Although their work is seldom read today, sisters Alice and Phoebe Cary of Cincinnati were popular poets in the mid-1800s. Alice Cary won wide praise for her poetry collections, including *Lyra and Other Poems*, as well as for her novels and essays. Phoebe Cary is chiefly remembered as the author of many beloved hymns.

The first Ohioan to earn a place among the nation's outstanding writers was William Dean Howells. Born in Martins Ferry in 1837,

Howells spent years working on newspapers in Dayton, Columbus, Jefferson, and other Ohio cities. In 1860, he left Ohio for Boston, where his writing earned the respect of the literary giants of the day. Howells's concern with the role of business in society is evident in his finest novels, *The Rise of Silas Lapham* and *A Hazard of New Fortunes*. He recalled his Ohio roots in a series of autobiographies, as well as in the novels *New Leaf Mills* and *The Leatherwood God*.

One of the first black writers to gain recognition in America was Charles W. Chesnutt. Though he lived most of this life in Cleveland, the years he spent in North Carolina furnished the background for his novels and short stories. His story collections *The Conjure Woman* and *The Wife of His Youth*, both published in 1899, offer vivid glimpses into rural black folk culture.

The son of a runaway slave, Paul Laurence Dunbar grew up in Dayton. Like Chesnutt, he set most of his novels and poems in the South. Many of his poems, such as "When Malindy Sings," are written in black dialect.

One November day in 1912, a paint dealer in Elyria suddenly announced to his secretary, "My feet are cold and wet. I have been walking for too long in the bed of a river." With these enigmatic words, Sherwood Anderson walked out of his office and into a new life. He left Ohio for Chicago, where he launched his career as a writer. In his classic short-story collection *Winesburg, Ohio*, Anderson drew on his memories of Clyde, the western Ohio town where he grew up. He populated Winesburg with an unforgettable gallery of characters: religious fanatics, drifters, and recluses who cling precariously to the fringes of respectable society. Anderson criticized the shallowness of middle-class conventions in such works as *Many Marriages* and *Dark Laughter*.

Louis Bromfield also used fiction to point out the flaws of

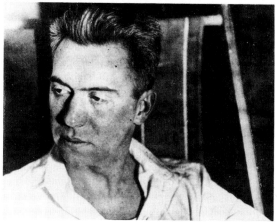

Three of Ohio's many important literary figures were poet and novelist Paul Laurence Dunbar (above), humorist James Thurber (top right), and poet Hart Crane (right).

modern society. In 1927, he won the Pulitzer Prize for *Early Autumn*, a novel about the struggles and triumphs of workers in an Ohio steel mill.

One of America's best-loved humorists, Columbus-born James Thurber, used wit to point out the foibles of urban life. In stories such as "The Secret Life of Walter Mitty," he showed modern man as a hapless victim who must escape into a world of fantasy. The eccentric relatives and improbable events of Thurber's childhood in Columbus fill the pages of *My Life and Hard Times* and *The Thurber Album*.

Two twentieth-century Ohio poets who left their mark on American literature were Hart Crane and James Wright. Hart Crane's epic poem *The Bridge* romanticizes the industrial age, tying it to the nation's legendary past. James Wright was haunted by the poverty and despair he saw in the coal-mining country around his hometown of Martins Ferry. "Autumn Comes to Martins Ferry, Ohio" is considered one of his finest poems. Wright's *Collected Poems* won the Pulitzer Prize in poetry in 1972.

Born in Lorain in 1931, Toni Morrison has earned a place of distinction among contemporary novelists. Her works examine the role of black people in American culture. Unlike Chesnutt and Dunbar, Morrison draws directly on the black experience in Ohio in several of her books, including *Beloved,* winner of the 1988 Pulitzer Prize in fiction.

ART

The names of many of Ohio's earliest artists have been lost to history. Some painted signs or decorated barges. Others carried bundles of half-finished portraits from town to town, ready to fill in the face when they found an eager customer.

The first Ohio portrait painter to earn national recognition was nineteenth-century artist Godfrey Frankenstein, who painted such notables as President John Quincy Adams and poet William Cullen Bryant. One of his contemporaries, Thomas D. Jones, sculpted many of the famous people of his day in marble, including William Henry Harrison and statesman Henry Clay. Jones's bust of Abraham Lincoln was commissioned for the state capitol in Columbus.

In 1837, a young artist from Cincinnati named Hiram Powers journeyed to Italy to study sculpture. Although he never returned to Ohio, several of his finest works eventually reached the Cincinnati Art Museum. The influence of his European training can be seen in such works as *Eve Disconsolate* and *Greek Slave.*

Above: *The Emancipated Slave*
by John Quincy Adams Ward
Right: A lithograph
copy of *The Spirit of '76* by
Archibald M. Willard

John Quincy Adams Ward, born near Urbana in 1830, rejected the classical style of painting in favor of simplicity and realism. His portraits are noted for their strong, pure lines. Ward also created life-size bronze sculptures. In works such as *Emancipated Slave*, he celebrates the dignity of ordinary human beings. His statue of James Garfield can be seen in Washington, D.C., and his *Indian Hunter* stands in New York City's Central Park.

Few people today recognize the name Archibald M. Willard, but his painting *The Spirit of '76* is part of the American consciousness. *The Spirit of '76*, painted for the nation's centennial celebration in 1876, depicts three generations of Revolutionary War soldiers. Through a haze of smoke, a drummer boy, a middle-aged piper with a bandaged head, and an elderly, white-haired drummer lead the Continental troops into battle.

Among the most influential American artists of the early twentieth century was Cincinnati-born Robert Henri. Henri believed that artists should paint realistically, without hiding the grimmer aspects of modern life. He became the leader of a group of New York painters referred to by their harsher critics as the Ashcan School.

Jim Dine of Cincinnati carries artistic experimentation even further. Dine's work is often controversial; he frequently attaches common household objects such as toothbrushes and garden tools to his painted canvases. A respected artist, Dine has won worldwide recognition among contemporary artists.

Other Ohio artists work to expand the horizons of artistic expression as well. At her studio outside Columbus, Nancy Crow creates beautiful quilts that rank as an art form. Using flashing lights and printed words, Jenny Holzer of Gallipolis combines language with visual art to convey her message.

Elijah Pierce, born in 1892, is one of the most noted folk artists in the United States. His wood sculptures and reliefs of animals, biblical scenes, and athletes have been exhibited in many major museums. The son of a former slave, Pierce left Mississippi for Ohio in the 1930s. His workshop and gallery in Columbus are on the National Register of Historic Places.

THE PERFORMING ARTS

A commitment to serious music in Ohio can be traced back more than a hundred years to the founding of the Oberlin Conservatory of Music in 1865 and the Cincinnati Conservatory in 1867. Cincinnatians enjoyed their first season of orchestral concerts in 1895, and by 1908, the Cincinnati Symphony Orchestra was permanently established. Today, the symphony performs regularly at the Cincinnati Music Hall, noted worldwide for its remarkable acoustics. The Music Hall also hosts the Cincinnati Ballet and an annual summer opera festival. Eden Park is the home of Cincinnati's Playhouse in the Park, a nationally acclaimed professional theater company.

Founded in 1918, the world-renowned Cleveland Orchestra has performed at Severance Hall since 1931. Hungarian-born conductor George Szell, who led the orchestra from 1946 to 1970, built it into one of the finest symphonies in the world. The Playhouse Square Center, a renovated three-theater complex, hosts the Cleveland Ballet and the Cleveland Opera. Among Cleveland's repertory companies are the Cleveland Play House, which presents plays at the Bolton, Brooks, and Drury theaters; and the Great Lakes Shakespeare Festival. Karamu House, opened in 1915 to promote racial understanding, uses integrated casting in plays by and about black Americans.

In the state capital, the Columbus Symphony Orchestra plays at the Ohio Theatre. Orchestras also perform in Dayton, Toledo, and Akron. Akron is also home to the Ohio Ballet Company.

SPORTS

Ohio State University at Columbus has one of the finest college sports programs in the country. When led by fiery coach Woody Hayes, the Ohio State Buckeyes football team dominated the Big Ten Conference. Hayes, whose teams won 238 games during his twenty-seven-year career, was known as much for his on-field temper outbursts as for his winning tradition. Ohio State has also produced notable basketball teams. Its squad in the early 1960s, which included Jerry Lucas and John Havlicek, is considered one of history's best college basketball teams.

Pro-football fans in northern Ohio follow the exploits of the Cleveland Browns, while the Cincinnati Bengals are most popular in the southern part of the state. One of football's greatest running

Every year, young people from all over the country come to Akron to compete in the All-American Soap Box Derby.

backs, Jim Brown, starred with Cleveland in the 1960s. The Bengals fielded a powerful team in the early 1980s that dazzled its foes with a precise passing attack.

Cleveland is home to a professional baskeball team, the Cleveland Cavaliers; and to an American League baseball team, the Cleveland Indians. Cincinnati's baseball team, the National League Cincinnati Reds, plays at Riverfront Stadium. Organized in 1869 as the Cincinnati Red Stockings, the Reds are baseball's oldest professional team. The Reds of the 1970s were called the "Big Red Machine" as they ran roughshod over their National League opponents. One of their stars—and later their manager— was Pete Rose, baseball's all-time leader in base hits.

Sometimes called the "golf capital of the world," Akron hosts the annual World Series of Golf. Every August, young people from all over the country bring their homemade cars to Akron to compete in the All-American Soap Box Derby.

One of the most extraordinary athletes the world has ever known was Jesse Owens. As a member of Ohio State's track and field team, Owens broke three world records in 1935. At the 1936 Olympic Games in Berlin, he won four gold medals. Owens's record in the broad jump stood unsurpassed for nearly thirty years.

Chapter 10

HIGHLIGHTS OF
THE BUCKEYE STATE

HIGHLIGHTS OF THE BUCKEYE STATE

It is sometimes said that Ohio is the "most American" of the states; a "state in the middle." It is not located in the middle of the country, but its history in many ways exemplifies the movements and trends that shaped the nation. A brief tour reveals forests and farmland, charming small towns, and teeming cities. A fascinating array of historical museums and monuments links the past to the present, recalling the men and women who helped build the Buckeye State.

MEMORIES OF PRESIDENTS

Ohio museums and monuments remind visitors of the many United States presidents who hailed from the Buckeye State. When eighteenth president Ulysses S. Grant was a boy, his father operated a tannery at Georgetown on Whiteoak Creek just north of the Ohio River. The two-room brick schoolhouse attended by Grant is now open to the public. Grant's birthplace in nearby Point Pleasant is also a revered Ohio landmark. The Rutherford B. Hayes Library and Museum State Memorial in Fremont includes exhibits on the life and times of the nineteenth president.

In Mentor, the twenty-six-room home of twentieth president James Garfield is open to the public. The house is furnished with many of Garfield's original possessions. In North Bend, the tomb of ninth American president William Henry Harrison is not far from the birthplace of his grandson, twenty-third president Benjamin Harrison.

The birthplace of President Ulysses S. Grant in Point Pleasant is among a number of sites in Ohio that honor the eight American presidents who hailed from the Buckeye State.

In 1896, William McKinley conducted his "front-porch" campaign for president from his home in the steel-making city of Canton. With his wife and two infant daughters, McKinley is buried within the McKinley Monument in Canton, a domed, hundred-foot- (thirty-meter-) tall granite mausoleum. Memorabilia of the twenty-fifth president's life and times are displayed at the McKinley Museum of the Stark County Historical Center. A national historic site in Cincinnati commemorates the career of twenty-seventh president William Howard Taft. The Warren G. Harding Home and Museum in Marion includes the twenty-ninth president's home, burial site, and the building where he edited the newspaper he owned before becoming president.

THE WESTERN PLAIN

The gently rolling plain of western Ohio contains some of the richest farmland in the country. The city of Dayton is surrounded by a patchwork of cornfields and pastures. Dayton is often called

A P-51 fighter plane on display at the United States Air Force Museum in Dayton

the "Birthplace of Aviation." During the 1890s, brothers Wilbur and Orville Wright operated a bicycle shop in Dayton while they tried to build the first successful flying machine. In 1903, they achieved their goal when they flew their first airplane at Kitty Hawk, North Carolina. Dayton continues to be an aircraft-manufacturing center. Wright-Patterson Air Force Base is not far from the field where the Wright brothers conducted their first experiments with flight. On the grounds of the base is the United States Air Force Museum, the world's largest and oldest military aviation museum. Also in Dayton is the restored home of poet Paul Laurence Dunbar.

Northwest of the city, at the junction of Loramie Creek and the Great Miami River, lies the Piqua Historical Area. This historic park marks the site of Fort Pickawillany, where the French and British once traded with the Indians and fought for control of the Ohio frontier. Visitors may examine artifacts in the Indian Museum, explore the restored 1815 home of Indian agent Colonel John Johnston, and ride a horse-drawn canal boat on a section of the old Miami and Erie Canal.

North of Dayton, the town of Wapakoneta celebrates its most famous native son, astronaut Neil Armstrong. The Neil

The restored nineteenth-century home of Indian agent John Johnston is part of the Piqua Historical Area.

Armstrong Air and Space Museum runs a continuous video of the Apollo 11 flight of July 20, 1969, when Armstrong became the first man to set foot on the moon. In the Astro Theater, the visitor is surrounded by the sights and sounds of a simulated space voyage.

North and west of Wapakoneta, near Van Wert, is a partial reconstruction of Fort Recovery. The original fort was built in 1793 by General Anthony Wayne and was used during the Indian wars in the Ohio region.

In northwest Ohio, near the edge of what was once the Black Swamp, lies the town of Findlay. In January 1886, drillers near Findlay struck a pocket of natural gas, and the Karg Well erupted into life. With a roar, a tower of flame shot 100 feet (31 meters) into the air. Heat from the burning gas melted the snow for half a mile (fourth-fifths of a kilometer) around. Findlay's gas boom lasted until 1890. Just when the gas wells began to run dry, oil deposits were discovered nearby. Findlay remained the headquarters of the Marathon Oil Company until the early 1980s.

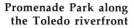

**Promenade Park along
the Toledo riverfront**

The Hancock Historical Museum-Hull House in Findlay features
an important glass collection that includes glass patterns produced
in Findlay in the 1880s.

THE LAKE SHORE

During the 1830s, Michigan and Ohio disputed the ownership
of the "Toledo Strip," a stretch of land along the western shore of
Lake Erie. In 1835, a band of Michiganders invaded Toledo, tore
down the Ohio flag, and dragged it through the streets. Congress
finally awarded Toledo and the rest of the land in question to
Ohio.

Since the early twentieth century, Toledo has been a major coal-
shipping center and manufacturer of auto parts. Despite setbacks
in heavy industry, downtown Toledo was renovated in the late
1970s and now boasts a complex of sparkling new high-rises
along elegant Promenade Park. Portside Festival Marketplace, a
huge, glass-enclosed shopping mall on the city's redeveloped
riverfront area, features more than seventy specialty shops,
restaurants, and vendors. The city's Old West End is graced by

Kelleys Island, one of several islands in Lake Erie along Ohio's North Coast, is a popular vacation spot.

magnificently restored Victorian mansions. The people of Toledo are especially proud of the Toledo Museum of Art, which houses a world-famous collection of works in glass.

A few miles outside of Toledo is Maumee, site of the Fallen Timbers State Memorial. At this site, in 1794, a decisive battle was fought between troops led by General Anthony Wayne and forces led by Miami Chief Little Turtle. Maumee is also home to the AAA minor-league Toledo Mud Hens baseball team.

Once home of the world's largest freshwater fish market, the city of Sandusky stands at the southern tip of Sandusky Bay. Cedar Point, a nearby amusement park, has offered thrilling rides and games of chance since 1882.

North of Sandusky Bay lies a cluster of islands, many of them popular summer resorts. Kelleys Island is famous for its boulders, which have clearly defined grooves cut by the movement of the great glaciers. One large boulder, Inscription Rock, contains markings that were carved by prehistoric Indians. The Perry's Victory and International Peace Memorial stands at Put-in-Bay on

South Bass Island. The 352-foot (107-meter) granite shaft—one of the nation's tallest—commemorates Commodore Oliver Hazard Perry's victory over the British fleet in the Battle of Lake Erie, fought off Sandusky Bay during the War of 1812. The monument also honors the enduring peace between the United States and Canada.

Less than an hour's drive away, in Milan, visitors can tour the birthplace of inventor Thomas Edison. Seven furnished rooms in the 1841 brick cottage display Edison's inventions and family furnishings. Nearby Norwalk is home to the Firelands Historical Society. This museum, the state's second-oldest, displays both pioneer and Indian artifacts.

Ohio's largest city, Cleveland, fans south from the lake across the S-shaped curves of the Cuyahoga River. The Flats, once a bleak landscape of warehouses and smokestacks along the riverbank, has gradually been transformed into a district of cafes, shops, nightclubs, and artists' lofts. The city's three main avenues converge downtown at the Public Square. The square is dominated by the forty-six-story Standard Oil Building, built in 1985; and the fifty-two-story Terminal Tower, the tallest building in Ohio. The Terminal Tower has been a Cleveland landmark since its completion in 1927.

Cleveland is the hub of culture in northern Ohio. The city claims one of the most heavily used public-library systems in the nation. The area around Case Western Reserve University, known as University Circle, is rich in cultural institutions. The Cleveland Museum of Art has an outstanding collection of American, Asian, and European works. Other museums of special interest on the Circle include the Cleveland Museum of Natural History, Ohio's largest natural-history museum; and the Western Reserve Historical Society, which traces the history of northeastern Ohio

Cleveland's Terminal Tower is the tallest building in Ohio.

in artifacts and pictures. The historical society is also known for its extensive genealogical collection.

The Heritage Park along the Cuyahoga River is also of historical interest, marking the site of Moses Cleaveland's original settlement of 1796. The cabin and trading center of Lorenzo Carter, one of Cleveland's first white inhabitants, has been rebuilt in the park. Above the park, the High Level Bridge arches over the river and affords a panoramic view of the city.

Cleveland is also home to a series of twenty-three unique mini-parks called culture gardens, which honor the contributions of various ethnic groups to the state and to the nation. The first

Severance Hall is the home of the world-renowned Cleveland Orchestra.

culture garden was created by the British in 1916. Today, parks celebrate Yugoslavians, Russians, Italians, Greeks, Germans, Poles, Rumanians, blacks, Chinese, and many other peoples.

Ohio's close ties to transportation are evident at three Cleveland attractions. The Crawford Auto-Aviation Museum houses more than two hundred restored vehicles. The NASA Lewis Research Center has a visitor's center with exhibits that detail the work of the National Aeronautics and Space Administration. The USS-*COD*, a docked World War II submarine, can be toured during the summer.

The greater Cleveland area is encircled by the "Emerald Necklace," a vast system of parklands covering 17,000 acres (6,880 hectares). The Emerald Necklace provides a respite from the stresses of city life with tennis courts, bicycle paths, a golf course, nature preserves, and a zoo.

EASTERN OHIO

South of Cleveland spreads the great industrial triangle of Youngstown, Akron, and Canton. For generations, families worked in Youngstown's steel mills. Youngstown suffered soaring unemployment in the late 1970s when the mills began to shut down. A similar crisis confronted Akron when the major rubber corporations stopped producing automobile tires in the city. To revitalize the downtown area, Akron has transformed a complex of Quaker Oats grain silos and mills into Quaker Square, a plaza of shops, hotels, and restaurants. The Railways of America Museum, which features the world's largest model-train display, is also located on the square. One of Akron's most spectacular landmarks is the Goodyear Air Dock, the largest building in the world constructed without interior supports.

Canton is hailed as the city where professional football was born. The Canton Bulldogs were original members of the Professional Football Association, founded in 1920. Their star player was Jim Thorpe, one of the most remarkable athletes in sports history. A statue of Jim Thorpe greets visitors to the Pro Football Hall of Fame. Opened in Canton in 1963, the hall of fame is crowned by a fifty-two-foot (sixteen-meter) football-shaped dome. With its football-action movie theater, research library, and galleries filled with mementos of famous players and games, the Football Hall of Fame is a sports fan's paradise. North Canton is home to an unusual display—antique and early vacuum cleaners—at the Hoover Historical Center.

Guides in eighteenth-century dress demonstrate frontier cooking, sewing, and candle making at Schoenbrunn Village near New Philadelphia. Much of the 1772 Moravian mission settlement has been reconstructed, including the schoolhouse and the

The Akron skyline

meetinghouse where church services were held. Cabins in various stages of completion reveal early building techniques. The historical play *Trumpet in the Land* dramatizes the events surrounding the first white settlement in Ohio. It is performed outdoors from May to September.

The area around New Philadelphia offered refuge for several religious groups. Zoar Village, a small settlement near New Philadelphia, preserves the eighteenth-century home of Joseph Bimeler, leader of a German religious sect that sought freedom from persecution. The settlement's gardens, first planted in the 1830s, are also on display. Berlin, a tiny town west of Sugar Creek, includes the Amish County Crafts Village, which features exhibits of Amish farm crafts.

Less than an hour's drive southwest of New Philadelphia is Roscoe Village at Coshocton. This restored 1830s community offers insights into life on the Ohio and Erie Canal during the early nineteenth century. Visitors to the village can take a boat ride in a horse-drawn canal boat.

Southeast of Coshocton, in the heart of a glassmaking region, is the town of Cambridge. The Cambridge Glass Museum houses the world's largest collection of Cambridge glass. Nearby is the

100

Degenhart Paperweight and Glass Museum, where exhibits focus on glassmaking techniques. Mosser Glass, also in Cambridge, offers tours of its glassmaking facilities.

Just outside Zanesville stands the National Road-Zane Grey Memorial Museum. A diorama re-creates the history of the National Road, once the major land route for pioneer families crossing Ohio. Authentic vehicles including a Conestoga wagon, early bicycles, and antique automobiles show the evolution of road transportation. The museum also houses a collection of papers, first editions, and other memorabilia of Zanesville-born Zane Grey, the immensely popular writer of western novels.

At the Ohio Ceramic Center between Crooksville and Roseville, three buildings brim with exhibits on the history of pottery making in the Buckeye State. Pottery is still a thriving industry in southern Ohio and in many towns along the Ohio River.

Rich deposits of bituminous coal lie beneath the knobby hills and narrow, twisting valleys of southern Ohio. Still largely rural, this region has been scarred by strip mining, but conservation programs have managed to reclaim much of the damaged land. A century of effort, however, has not succeeded in extinguishing the New Straitsville Fire. In the frenzy of a labor strike in 1884, angry miners set five wagons of coal ablaze and rolled them into a deep underground mine. The veins of coal fed the insatiable flames. After more than a hundred years, the fire still smolders in the maze of tunnels beneath New Straitsville.

ALONG THE OHIO

Many of the Buckeye State's most fascinating towns and cities lie along the northern bank of the Ohio River. Steubenville, not far from the Pennsylvania border, was the site of Fort Steuben, built in 1787 to protect government surveyors from Indian attack. The town of La Belle grew up around the fort, predating Marietta by several months. But La Belle was abandoned in 1790, making Marietta Ohio's first permanent white settlement.

Marietta, today a charming college town with broad streets and Victorian houses, is steeped in history. The Campus Martius Museum contains a scale model of the original settlement and three galleries of paintings and artifacts that trace the development of early Ohio. The home of Rufus Putnam, leader of the 1787 settlement, has been carefully restored. Nearby stands the original cabin that once served as a land office for the Northwest Territory. The Ohio River Museum in Marietta brings the era of the steamboat vividly to life with pictures, steam whistles, and even an authentic stern-wheeler.

Although commercial steamboats disappeared from the Ohio in the 1880s, Cincinnati is still home port to the *Delta Queen* and the *Mississippi Queen*. These two splendidly restored steamboats continue to ply their way down the Ohio and the Mississippi, introducing travelers to the lore of the river. The blasts of their steam whistles as they wind along the Ohio's twists and curves evoke the ghosts of the majestic vessels that rode the currents when steamboat travel was at its height.

Cincinnati's central business district stands in the "Basin," a flat plain extending from the riverfront and embraced by a semicircle of seven hills. Fountain Square, named for its bronze fountain imported from Munich in 1871, is the hub of downtown Cincinnati. Major renovations during the 1960s graced downtown with a gleaming modern convention center complete with banks, restaurants, and shops of every variety.

Cincinnati supports many excellent museums. The Cincinnati Art Museum contains ancient and modern works from all over

Cincinnati scenes

A fireworks display over the Ohio River in Cincinnati

the world. It is particularly noted for its unique collections of Near Eastern and American Indian art. Other fine art collections are housed at the Contemporary Arts Center in the convention center, and at the Taft Museum, known for its Northern European art.

One of the most fascinating exhibits at the Cincinnati Museum of Natural History is the Cavern. In this section of the museum, visitors explore full-sized replicas of portions of several caves in Ohio and Kentucky. The Cavern displays samples of such underground formations as stalactites and stalagmites, and even features a thirty-foot (nine-meter) waterfall.

The loss of thousands of manufacturing jobs has contributed to poverty in Cincinnati's inner-city neighborhoods, especially among blacks and white migrants from Appalachia. Despite its problems, however, Cincinnati has left the days of "Boss" Cox far behind. A series of reforms has built a city government known throughout the nation for its efficiency and honesty.

THE MIDDLE OF THE MIDDLE STATE

In order to please people throughout the state, Ohio's early legislators located the permanent capital—Columbus—at almost the exact center of the state. At the center of Capital Square in the heart of the city stands the state capitol, an imposing limestone structure flanked by Greek columns on each of its four entrances. A cluster of bronze statues on the capitol grounds honors seven Ohioans who served their country during and after the Civil War: General and President Ulysses S. Grant, General William T. Sherman, General Philip H. Sheridan, President James A. Garfield, President Rutherford B. Hayes, Secretary of War Edwin M. Stanton, and Supreme Court Justice Salmon P. Chase.

Sprawling over 184 square miles (477 square kilometers), Columbus covers more area than any other Ohio city. In fact, Columbus is one of the largest cities in area in the United States. Manufacturing, state government, and Ohio State University provide thousands of jobs in the city.

The headquarters of the Battelle Memorial Institute, one of the largest nonprofit scientific research institutes in the world, are located in Columbus. The Battelle Planetarium at the Center of Science and Industry gives visitors a stunning view of a simulated sky. Among the center's other fascinating exhibits is a replica of a coal mine.

South of downtown Columbus lies German Village, a restored community containing five hundred homes built between 1840 and 1860. Every June, German Village invites the public for a special Haus and Garten (house and garden) Tour. Another reconstructed community in Columbus is Ohio Village, where visitors can enjoy an authentically prepared nineteenth-century meal. The adjacent Ohio Historical Center is a treasure trove of

The Cultural Arts
Center in Columbus

displays about the state's history and growth. Four shelves in the
historical center's library hold the famous Coonskin Library, one
of Ohio's earliest collections of books. In the early 1800s, residents
of what is now Amesville purchased these books with bear hides,
wolf hides, and raccoon skins.

The area surrounding Columbus is another history-rich region
of Ohio. East of the capital is Newark, home of Johnny Clem, the
Civil War hero known as "Johnny Shiloh." The engineering feats
of some of Ohio's earliest people can still be seen at the Newark
Earthworks. Remnants of a great, man-made, octagonal ridge
enclose the fifty-acre (twenty-hectare) site of an ancient village.

More evidence of Ohio's early inhabitants is visible in the
mounds around Chillicothe. The Mound City Group National
Monument there includes twenty-three burial mounds

106

constructed about two thousand years ago by people of the Hopewell Culture. The famous Great Serpent Mound lies about an hour's drive south of the Mound City Group.

Chillicothe's first white settlers were farmers from Virginia who received grants of land for their service during the Revolutionary War. The town became the capital of the Northwest Territory in 1800, and served as Ohio's first state capital in 1803. Adena State Memorial preserves the plantation home of Thomas Worthington, Ohio's sixth governor. During the summer months, Chillicothe presents an outdoor historical drama, *Tecumseh!*, which depicts the life of the great Indian leader.

Throughout the year, and throughout the state, festivals and fairs highlight the diversity of Ohio's people. Cleveland, Steubenville, Lima, Jackson, and other cities host such annual ethnic song festivals as the Welsh Eisteddfod and the German Saengerfest. Other activities in the state mark the contributions of immigrants from Ireland, Hungary, Bohemia, Switzerland, and Scandinavia. A multitude of events in the state celebrate the abundance of the land. In early spring, Oxford, Chardon, and Geauga hold maple-syrup festivals. The Ohio State Fair, held each year in Columbus, proudly displays the best examples of dairying, livestock, and crops the state has to offer. Apples in Jackson and pumpkins in Circleville mark autumn in the state, and winter brings ice fishing on Lake Erie and skiing parties in Akron and Bellefontaine.

In all, a tour of Ohio shows visitors that this midwestern state has a rich heritage of people and history, a strong industrial footing, and a prosperous relation with the land. With assets such as these, the state's motto, With God, All Things Are Possible, rings clear and true indeed.

FACTS AT A GLANCE

GENERAL INFORMATION

Statehood: March 1, 1803, seventeenth state

Origin of Name: Named for the Ohio River; the word *Ohio* comes from the Iroquois word *oheo,* variously translated as "something great," "great river," or "beautiful"

State Capital: Columbus

State Nickname: "Buckeye State"

State Flag: Ohio's flag is the nation's only pennant-shaped state flag. It has three red and two white horizontal stripes, and a blue triangular field with seventeen stars representing Ohio's entrance into the Union as the seventeenth state. Within the triangle, a red disc, symbolizing the buckeye nut, is surrounded by a white "o," symbolizing the initial letter of the state's name.

State Motto: With God, All Things Are Possible

State Bird: Cardinal

State Flower: Scarlet carnation

State Tree: Buckeye

State Stone: Ohio flint

State Insect: Ladybug

State Fossil: Isotelus (trilobite)

State Beverage: Tomato juice

State Song: "Beautiful Ohio," words by Ballard MacDonald, music by Mary Earl; adopted in 1969:

Long, long ago, some one I know
Had a little red canoe, in it room for only two
Love found its start, then in my heart
And like a flower grew:

Drifting with the current down a moon-lit stream
While above the Heavens in their glory gleam
And the stars on high, twinkle in the sky
Seeming in a paradise of love divine
Dreaming of a pair of eyes that looked in mine.

Beautiful Ohio, in dreams again I see
Visions of what used to be.

POPULATION

Population: 10,797,624, sixth among the states (1980 census)

Population Density: 261 persons per sq. mi. (101 per km²)

Population Distribution: 73 percent of the people live in cities or towns. Cleveland is Ohio's largest city. Nearly one-fifth of all Ohioans live in Cleveland's sprawling metropolitan area along Lake Erie. The Columbus and Cincinnati metropolitan areas are each home to more than one million people.

Cleveland	573,822
Columbus	565,032
Cincinnati	385,457
Toledo	354,635
Akron	237,177
Dayton	193,444
Youngstown	115,436
Canton	93,077
Parma	92,548

(Population figures according to 1980 census)

Population Growth: Ohio's population increased fivefold in the few years between statehood in 1803 and a preliminary census in 1810. Between 1810 and 1820, the population doubled. The newcomers were land-hungry settlers from the older eastern-seaboard states. In the 1820s and 1830s, immigrants arrived from

Europe. Southern and eastern Europeans flocked to Ohio's industrial cities to find work after 1880. Blacks from the southern states came in large numbers to seek jobs in Ohio's industries during the Civil War period and after World War I. But the industrial slowdown of the 1970s also slowed down Ohio's population growth. Between 1970 and 1980, Ohio's population increased only 1.3 percent, while the population of the entire country increased 11.45 percent. The list below shows the official national census figures for Ohio since 1810:

Year	Population
1810	230,760
1820	581,434
1840	1,519,467
1860	2,339,511
1880	3,198,062
1900	4,157,545
1920	5,759,394
1940	6,907,612
1950	7,946,627
1960	9,706,397
1970	10,657,423
1980	10,797,624

GEOGRAPHY

Borders: States that border Ohio are Michigan on the north, Pennsylvania and West Virginia on the east, West Virginia and Kentucky on the south, and Indiana on the west. Nearly three-fourths of Ohio's northern border is formed by Lake Erie. The International Line between Canada and the United States passes through Lake Erie about 20 mi. (32 km) north of the Ohio shore.

Highest Point: Campbell Hill in Logan County, 1,550 ft. (472 m) above sea level

Lowest Point: Where the Ohio and Miami rivers meet, in Hamilton County, 433 ft. (132 m) above sea level

Greatest Distances: North to south—210 mi. (338 km)
East to west—230 mi. (370 km)

Area: 41,330 sq. mi. (107,045 km^2)

Rank in Area Among the States: Thirty-fifth

Rivers: A series of long, low hills runs diagonally across Ohio from the northeast corner of the state to Marion County along the western border. This ridge separates the state into two drainage regions. Rivers north and west of the ridge flow into Lake Erie and drain about one-third of the state. The major rivers that drain into

Lake Erie are the Maumee, Portage, Sandusky, Cuyahoga, Huron, Vermilion, and Grand. The land south and east of the ridge—the remaining two-thirds of Ohio—is drained by rivers that flow into the Ohio River. These rivers include the Great Miami, Little Miami, Scioto, Hocking, Tuscarawas, and Muskingum. The Ohio River, the state's most important river, winds some 450 mi. (724 km) to form the state's southern and southeastern borders. In all, Ohio has some thirty-three hundred named streams.

Lakes: Ohio has some twenty-five hundred lakes, of which only about 10 percent are natural lakes. Grand Lake, which covers 12,700 acres (5,140 hectares), is the largest lake lying wholly within the state. It was created in the 1840s to feed water into the Miami and Erie Canal. Pymatuning Reservoir, another large artificial lake, is shared by Ohio and Pennsylvania. Ohio's other large man-made lakes include Berlin, Indian, Mosquito Creek, and Senecaville lakes. In addition, Ohio's lake waters include 3,457 sq. mi. (8,954 km^2) of Lake Erie.

Topography: Ohio consists of three main land regions: the Great Lakes Plains in the north, the Allegheny Plateau in the east, and the Till Plain in the west.

The Great Lakes Plain region is part of the lowlands that line the shores of the Great Lakes. In Ohio, the region covers the northern part of the state in a fanlike strip that is only 5 to 10 mi. (8 to 16 km) wide in the east, but widens to more than 50 mi. (80 km) in the western part of the state. The level or slightly rolling plains were once covered by Lake Erie, and parts of the area remained nearly uncrossable swampland when white settlers arrived. The great Black Swamp, in northwestern Ohio around Toledo, was a major barrier to travel and settlement until it was drained. Today, the deep, fertile soil supports a variety of crops.

The Allegheny Plateau covers most of the eastern half of Ohio, curving westward from just below Lake Erie to the Ohio River. Many rivers wind through its steep hills. Glaciers sculpted the northern third of the region into rolling hills and valleys. The southern two-thirds of the plateau, untouched by glaciers, includes some of Ohio's most ruggedly beautiful scenery. The state's richest mineral deposits—coal, natural gas, oil, clay, and salt—are found in the Allegheny Plateau.

The Till Plain covers western Ohio from the Great Lakes Plain south to the Ohio River. Both the highest and the lowest elevations in the state are found here. In this region, gently rolling plains that contain the rich soil of the midwestern Corn Belt support the production of soybeans, grain, and livestock.

Climate: Ohio enjoys a generally temperate climate with warm, humid summers, cold winters, and large seasonal temperature changes. Cleveland, in the northeast, has an average July temperature of 74° F. (23° C) and an average January temperature of 28.5° F. (-2° C). Cincinnati, in the southeast, experiences somewhat warmer temperatures, averaging 76° F. (24° C) in July and 33° F. (0.5° C) in January. Ohio's highest recorded temperature of 113° F. (45° C) at Thurman on July 4, 1897 was matched near Gallipolis on July 21, 1934. Ohio's lowest recorded temperature, -39° F. (-39° C), occurred at Milligan on February 10, 1899. Ohio's average annual precipitation (rain, melted snow, and other moisture) is 38 in. (97 cm).

The sugar maple is one of the many kinds of trees found in Ohio.

NATURE

Trees: White ash, basswood, beech, birch, buckeye, butternut, elm, hemlock, hickory, locust, bigleaf magnolia, maple, oak, pine, poplar, sourwood, sycamore, walnut, tulip, wild cherry

Wild Plants: Ohio's more than 2,000 species of wild plants include anemones, azaleas, blazing stars, blue sages, hawthorn, hornbeam, Indian pipes, lilies, pawpaw, sassafras, saxifrages, toothworts, viburnum, wild indigos, and witch hazel. The state has some 200 threatened and endangered species, including the yellow-fringed orchid, white-painted trillium, and white lady's slipper.

Animals: Badgers, beavers, bobcats, coyotes, deer, foxes, minks, moles, muskrats, opossums, rabbits, shrews, skunks, snakes, squirrels, woodchucks, salamanders, turtles, frogs, toads

Birds: Blackbirds, cardinals, chickadees, cowbirds, mourning doves, ducks, geese, grouse, herons, kingfishers, larks, pheasants, quail, teals, thrashers, warblers, woodpeckers, wrens

Fish: Ohio boasts some 170 species of fish, including bass, bluegills, catfish, darters, muskellunge, perch, pickerel, pike, suckers, and trout.

GOVERNMENT

The state government of Ohio, like the federal government, is divided into three branches: legislative, judicial, and executive.

The legislative branch, or General Assembly, consists of a thirty-three-member senate and a ninety-nine-member house of representatives. State senators are elected to four-year terms; state representatives are elected to two-year terms. The General Assembly makes new laws and determines how state revenue will be spent.

The judicial branch, which interprets the law, consists of a supreme court, courts of appeals, and lower courts. The supreme court consists of six justices and a chief justice who are elected by the people to six-year terms. Appeals courts have at least three members; in the more-populous counties they may have more. Each of Ohio's eighty-eight counties has a lower court, or court of common pleas. Judges in these courts are elected to six-year terms.

The executive branch carries out the law. The governor of Ohio is elected to a four-year term and may serve an unlimited number of terms, but no more than two consecutive terms. The governor appoints the heads of many state departments, has the power to veto legislation, and serves as commander-in-chief of the state militia.

Number of Counties: 88

U.S. Representatives: 21

Electoral Votes: 23

Voting Qualifications: Eighteen years of age or older, United States citizen, thirty-day residency

EDUCATION

Ohio's 616 public-school districts have a total enrollment of about 1.8 million pupils, with one teacher for every 18.3 students. About 40 percent of the state's budget is spent on education.

College and university enrollment approximates 400,000 students, 75 percent of whom are enrolled in public institutions. The state's largest public university is Ohio State University, which enrolls more than fifty thousand students at its main campus in Columbus. Ohio State also has branches in Lima, Mansfield, Marion, and Newark. Other public colleges and universities include Bowling Green State University; Central State University, in Wilberforce; University of Cincinnati; Cleveland State University; Kent State University; Miami University, in Oxford; Ohio University, in Athens; the University of Akron; the University of Toledo; Wright State University, in Dayton; and Youngstown State University.

Among Ohio's many private colleges and universities are Antioch College, in Yellow Springs; Baldwin Wallace College, in Berea; Case Western Reserve University, in Cleveland; the University of Dayton; Kenyon College, in Gambier; Denison University, in Granville; Ohio Wesleyan University, in Delaware; and Xavier University, in Cincinnati. Oberlin College was the nation's first coeducational college. Wilberforce University was the nation's first permanent private college established for blacks.

ECONOMY AND INDUSTRY

Principal Products:
Agriculture: Beef cattle, corn, dairy products, hay, hogs, poultry, sheep, soybeans, winter wheat
Manufacturing: Automobiles, trucks, truck trailers, airplane and motor-vehicle parts, machine tools, construction machinery, industrial machinery, cash registers, chemicals, electrical machinery and equipment, fabricated metal products, farm machinery, food products, clay and glass products, heating and cooling equipment, motorcycles, paper products, plastics, primary metals, printed materials, rubber products
Natural Resources: Clay, coal, gypsum, limestone, natural gas, petroleum, salt, sandstone, stone

Business and Trade: Ohio produces a wide variety of goods and is one of the nation's leading manufacturing states. Fifty-three of the nation's five hundred largest corporations have their headquarters in Ohio. Among them are such giants as Proctor & Gamble Company, in Cincinnati; Goodyear Tire & Rubber Company, in Akron; National Cash Register Company, in Dayton; Firestone Tire & Rubber Company, in Akron; Sherwin-Williams Company, in Cleveland; and Champion Sparkplug Company, in Toledo.

Communication: About 100 daily newspapers are published in Ohio. The *Plain Dealer* of Cleveland has the largest circulation. Other leading newspapers include the *Columbus Dispatch*, the *Dayton News/Journal Herald*, the *Cincinnati Enquirer*, the *Blade* of Toledo, the *Akron Beacon Journal*, and the *Cincinnati Post*. Ohio has approximately 285 radio stations and 50 television stations.

Transportation: Ohio has 775 airfields and is served by about 20 airlines. Cleveland's Hopkins International Airport is Ohio's busiest airport. Cincinnati, Columbus, and Dayton are also served by international airports. Cleveland, on Lake Erie and the St. Lawrence Seaway, is a major shipping port for iron ore. Other important port cities are Cincinnati and Toledo. Ohio has about 112,000 mi. (180,242 km) of roads and highways. About ten Ohio cities are served by passenger trains, and four railroads haul freight over approximately 6,600 mi. (10,622 km) of track.

The Columbus Museum of Art

SOCIAL AND CULTURAL LIFE

Museums: Ohio has more than three hundred museums, including eleven major art museums, twenty smaller art museums, and more than fifty college and university galleries. The Cleveland Museum of Art has more than forty-five thousand art objects. The Cleveland Museum of Natural History is Ohio's largest natural-science museum. The Cleveland Children's Museum features many hands-on exhibits. The Cincinnati Art Museum is particularly noted for its Near Eastern and American Indian Art and for its Greek and Roman statues. The Cincinnati Museum of Natural History includes a giant cavern complete with a 30-ft. (9-m) waterfall, stalactites, and other cave formations. The Columbus Museum of Art is noted for its outdoor sculpture garden, which features nineteenth- and twentieth-century American and European works. Also in Columbus is the Center of Science and Industry, a technology museum that includes a planetarium and a replica of a coal mine. The Toledo Museum of Art is renowned for its exhibits of glass from around the world. The Dayton Art Museum and the Akron Art Museum both have large permanent collections.

The main reference room of the Cleveland Public Library

Specialized museums include the Western Reserve Historical Society Museum in Cleveland, which traces the history of northeastern Ohio in artifacts and pictures; The Rock and Roll Hall of Fame, also in Cleveland; and the Taft Museum in Cincinnati, noted for its Chinese porcelains. The Butler Institute of American Art in Youngstown is devoted exclusively to American art, with more than four thousand works from colonial times to the present. The United States Air Force Museum at Wright-Patterson Air Force Base near Dayton is the world's largest military aviation museum.

Libraries: Ohio has about 250 public libraries, 10 library systems, and about 400 branch libraries. The Public Library of Cincinnati and Hamilton County, with more than 3.4 million volumes, is the state's largest. The Cleveland Public Library, with 2.5 million volumes, is the second-largest library system. Columbus and Dayton each have more than 1 million volumes in their public libraries. Ohio State University in Columbus and the University of Cincinnati have the largest academic libraries. The State Library of Ohio is in Columbus. In 1916, the library of the Rutherford B. Hayes Presidential Center in Fremont became the nation's first presidential library.

Pete Rose, who played for and later managed the Cincinnati Reds, is baseball's all-time leader in base hits.

Performing Arts: Ohio has approximately 72 symphony orchestras, including the nationally ranked Cincinnati Symphony Orchestra, established in 1908; and the world-renowned Cleveland Orchestra, which rose to international preeminence under the direction of the late George Szell. In the summer, the Cleveland Orchestra gives concerts at the Blossom Music Center near Cuyahoga Falls. Columbus, Dayton, and Toledo also have professional orchestras. Ohio is home to 28 major dance companies, including the Cleveland Ballet, the Cincinnati Ballet, and the Ohio Ballet Company of Akron. Columbus, Cincinnati, and Cleveland have opera companies. Ohio has 7 professional theater companies, approximately 150 community theaters, 9 children's theaters, and 54 college and university theaters. The Cleveland Play House is one of America's oldest resident theater companies. Karamu House, also in Cleveland, was founded in 1915 with the aim of bridging black and white cultures through the arts.

Sports and Recreation: Ohio has five major-league professional sports teams. Major-league baseball is played at Riverfront Stadium, home of the National League Cincinnati Reds; and at Cleveland Stadium, home of the American League Cleveland Indians. Riverfront Stadium is also the home of the Cincinnati Bengals of the National Football League. Cleveland Stadium is home to the NFL's Cleveland Browns. The Cleveland Cavaliers of the National Basketball Association play their home games at Ritchfield Coliseum.

In collegiate sports, the Ohio State Buckeyes are a perennial powerhouse in football, basketball, and other sports. The University of Cincinnati, Xavier University, the University of Dayton, and Cleveland State University also have strong basketball teams that enjoy wide followings.

Fort Meigs State Memorial features a reconstruction of a log fort built during the War of 1812.

With more than seventy state parks, nineteen state forests, and one national forest, Ohio provides nearly endless opportunities for outdoor activities. Swimming, boating, fishing, hunting, horseback riding, canoeing, and waterskiing are just a few of the possibilities. Ohio's many caves are a spelunker's delight. Popular game fish include walleye, perch, and smallmouth bass. Winter sports include ice fishing, skating, cross-country skiing, and snowmobiling.

Ohio has several large amusement parks. Cedar Point on Lake Erie is a huge amusement park featuring fifty-four exciting rides, theaters, animals and animal attractions, and a stretch of sandy beach. Sea World near Geauga Lake has marine shows and exhibits that feature whales, dolphins, penguins, otters, sharks, and other marine life.

Historic Sites and Landmarks:

Adena State Memorial, near Chillicothe, is the restored 1807 mansion of Thomas Worthington, Ohio's sixth governor.

Dunbar House State Memorial, in Dayton, is the restored home of famed poet Paul Laurence Dunbar.

Fort Ancient, southeast of Lebanon, preserves prehistoric Indian earthworks and includes a museum with exhibits on the Hopewell and Fort Ancient cultures.

Fort Laurens State Memorial, near Bolivar, is a museum at the site of the only American Revolution fort in Ohio. Just outside the museum is the Tomb of the Unknown Patriot of the American Revolution.

Fort Meigs State Memorial, in Perrysburg, is one of the largest reconstructed walled forts in America. The fort houses exhibits about the War of 1812.

Fort Recovery, in the town of Fort Recovery, is the partly reconstructed 1793 fort of General Anthony Wayne. The site includes a museum.

Grant's Birthplace State Memorial, in Point Pleasant, is the restored home of Ulysses S. Grant, Civil War hero and eighteenth president of the United States.

Warren G. Harding Home and Museum, Memorial, and the Star Building, in Marion, include the restored home of Warren G. Harding, twenty-ninth president of the United States; Harding's tomb, a Greek Revival-style memorial; and the building where Harding edited his newspaper.

Harrison Tomb State Memorial, in North Bend, is the final resting place of William Henry Harrison, ninth president of the United States.

Rutherford B. Hayes Library and Museum State Memorial, in Fremont, is a museum, library, and the former home of Rutherford B. Hayes, nineteenth president of the United States.

Lawnfield, in Mentor, is a twenty-six-room house that once belonged to James A. Garfield, twentieth president of the United States.

McKinley Monument, in Canton, honors William McKinley, twenty-fifth president of the United States.

Moundbuilders Earthworks, in Newark, is a complex of geometric mounds built by people of the Hopewell culture.

Mound City Group National Monument, near Chillicothe, preserves twenty-three prehistoric Hopewell burial mounds.

Perry's Victory and International Peace Memorial National Monument, on South Bass Island, commemorates Commodore Oliver Perry's victory over the British in the Battle of Lake Erie during the War of 1812.

Serpent Mound State Monument, near Hillsboro, preserves the largest serpent effigy mound in the United States. Built by the ancient Adena people to resemble a snake, the 1300-ft.- (396-m-) long mound contains seven sharp curves.

William Howard Taft National Historic Site, in Cincinnati, preserves the early home of William Howard Taft, the twenty-seventh president of the United States.

Other Interesting Places to Visit:

Neil Armstrong Air and Space Museum, in Wapakoneta, celebrates the history of aviation and aerospace development, including the historic flight of Apollo 11.

Historic Lyme Village, in Bellevue, is a collection of buildings from the 1700s and 1800s; featured are demonstrations of a variety of early American crafts.

A replica of the ancient pictographs carved into Inscription Rock on Kelleys Island

Kelleys Island, in Lake Erie near Sandusky, is a popular vacation spot. It is noted for the unusual glacial grooves cut into its rocks and for Inscription Rock, a huge limestone boulder etched with pictographs carved by prehistoric Indians.

Ohio Caverns, near West Liberty, are the largest and some of the most beautiful limestone caves in Ohio.

Pro Football Hall of Fame, in Canton, honors professional football's greatest players.

Schoenbrunn Village, near New Philadelphia, is a reconstruction of a 1772 Moravian mission. Its eighteen log structures include Ohio's first schoolhouse.

State Capitol, in Columbus, is a Greek Revival structure that has been a Columbus landmark since 1861.

Stowe House, in Cincinnati, is a black-history center that was the former home of Harriet Beecher Stowe, famed abolitionist and author of *Uncle Tom's Cabin.*

Wright-Patterson Air Force Base, near Dayton, contains the world's oldest and largest military aviation museum, as well as the field where the Wright brothers first experimented with airplanes.

Zoar Village, near Canton, is a restoration of a village built in 1817 by a small group of German Separatists.

IMPORTANT DATES

c. 700 B.C.—People of the Adena Culture begin building mounds in what is now southern Ohio

c. 100 B.C.-A.D. 500—The mound-building Hopewell Culture flourishes throughout the Ohio Valley

c. 1669—René-Robert Cavelier, Sieur de La Salle, is believed to have passed through the region between Lake Erie and the Ohio River, thus becoming the first white man to reach what is now Ohio

1747—The Ohio Company of Virginia is formed and given a provisional grant of land on the Ohio River

1749—French explorer Céloron de Bienville buries a series of lead plates along the Ohio River and claims the entire region for France

1763—France gives up its claim on the Ohio region to Great Britain

1772—David Zeisberger founds a Moravian mission settlement at Schoenbrunn

1787—The Northwest Territory is established

1788—Rufus Putnam and a group of forty-eight pioneers establish the first permanent white settlement in Ohio at Marietta

1794—Troops led by General Anthony Wayne defeat forces led by Little Turtle in the Battle of Fallen Timbers, ending Indian resistance in the Ohio region

1795—Treaty of Greenville brings a formal close to the Indian wars; the Indians cede two-thirds of present-day Ohio to the United States

1796—General Moses Cleaveland and his surveyors lay out a town site that will become Cleveland

1800—Congress divides the Northwest Territory into two parts; the eastern part— the land of present-day Ohio—continues to be called the Northwest Territory; Chillicothe is named the territorial capital

1803—Ohio becomes the seventeenth state

1810—Zanesville becomes the state capital

1811—The *New Orleans* becomes the first steamboat to travel down the Ohio River

1812—The state capital is moved from Zanesville to Chillicothe

A barge on an Ohio canal in the late 1800s

1813—American forces under Commodore Oliver H. Perry defeat the British in the Battle of Lake Erie

1816—Columbus is made the permanent state capital

1832—The Ohio and Erie Canal, connecting Cleveland and Portsmouth, is completed

1833—Oberlin College, the nation's first coeducational college and one of the first to welcome students "without respect to color," is founded

1836—Congress settles the boundary dispute between Ohio and Michigan, thus ending the "Toledo War"

1840—William Henry Harrison becomes the first Ohio resident elected president of the United States

1845—The Miami and Erie Canal, connecting Toledo and Cincinnati, is completed

1851—Present state constitution is adopted

1863—Confederate general John Hunt Morgan leads a group of cavalrymen known as Morgan's Raiders into Ohio; they are captured by Union troops at Salineville

1868—Ulysses S. Grant becomes the first native-born Ohioan to be elected president of the United States

1869—The Cincinnati Red Stockings (now called the Reds) become the nation's first professional baseball team

1880—Ohioan James A. Garfield is elected president of the United States

1888—Ohioan Benjamin Harrison is elected president of the United States

1894—"Coxey's Army," led by Jacob S. Coxey, marches from Massillon to Washington, D.C. to dramatize unemployment and poverty

1896—Ohioan William McKinley is elected president of the United States

1903—At Kitty Hawk, North Carolina, the Wright brothers of Dayton make the first successful flight in a self-propelled, heavier-than-air machine; Barney Oldfield achieves the (then) incredible speed of 60 mi. (97 km) per hour in his racing car

1908—Ohioan William Howard Taft is elected president of the United States

1912—The state constitution is amended extensively during the fourth constitutional convention

1913—Devastating floods in Ohio kill 430 people and cause $250 million worth of property damage

1914—The Ohio legislature passes the Conservancy Act to provide for the creation of major flood-control measures

1917-18—More than 250,000 Ohio men and women serve in the armed forces during World War I

1920—Ohioan Warren G. Harding is elected president of the United States

1922—Ohioan Florence E. Allen becomes the first woman in the United States to serve as a state supreme court justice; the Miami River Valley flood-control project is completed

1925—Ohioan Charles Gates Dawes wins the Nobel Peace Prize

1936—Jesse Owens of Ohio State University wins four gold medals in the Olympic Games at Berlin, Germany

1938—The Muskingum River Valley flood-control project is completed

1941-45—Nearly 840,000 Ohio men and women serve in the armed forces during World War II

1955—The Ohio Turnpike is opened to traffic

1962—Ohioan John Glenn becomes the first American to orbit the earth

1967—Carl Stokes is elected mayor of Cleveland, becoming the first black mayor of a major American city; voters approve a reapportionment plan for the state legislature

1969—Ohioan Neil Armstrong becomes the first man to walk on the moon; a heavy oil slick on the Cuyahoga River catches fire

1970—Four students are killed by National Guard troops during antiwar demonstrations at Kent State University

1971—Ohio adopts its first state income tax

1985—Western Ohio suffers a tornado that causes 12 deaths and $3.5 million worth of property damage; Governor Richard Celeste closes 71 state insured banks and savings-and-loan associations after a bank run in Cincinnati

1988—The collapse of an oil tank spills nearly a million gal. (3.8 million l) of diesel fuel into the Monongahela and Ohio rivers, creating a huge oil slick

IMPORTANT PEOPLE

Sherwood Anderson (1876-1941), born in Camden; writer; best known for *Winesburg, Ohio*, a group of stories about small-town life

Neil Alden Armstrong (1930-   ), born in Wapakoneta; astronaut; commanded Apollo 11, landed its lunar module, and became the first person to set foot on the moon on July 20, 1969; professor of engineering at the University of Cincinnati (1971-79)

SHERWOOD ANDERSON

Theda Bara (1885-1955), born Theodosia Goodman in Cincinnati; silent-film actress; best known for creating the image of the "vamp" in such films as *Salome* and *Cleopatra*

Joseph Brant (1742-1807), Ohio-born Mohawk leader; translated the *Episcopal Prayer Book* into the Mohawk language; led Indian forces on the side of the British during the Revolutionary War

Eliza Bryant (1827-1907), social reformer; worked in Cleveland to establish institutions to support the needs of elderly blacks; through her efforts, the Home for Aged Colored People (renamed in her honor in 1960) was established

JOSEPH BRANT

SALMON CHASE

CHARLES CHESNUTT

CLARENCE DARROW

CHARLES GATES DAWES

Alice Cary (1820-1871), born near Cincinnati; poet; published a number of poetry collections, including (with her sister Phoebe) *Poems of Alice and Phoebe Cary*

Phoebe Cary (1824-1871), born near Cincinnati; poet; sister of Alice Cary; best known for her hymn "Nearer Home"

John Chapman (1774-1845), nicknamed Johnny Appleseed; pioneer, folk hero; planted some 1,200 acres (486 hectares) of orchard, especially apple trees, as he roamed the Ohio Valley

Salmon Portland Chase (1808-1873), lawyer, politician, jurist; defended fugitive slaves; U.S. senator from Ohio (1849-55, 1860); governor of Ohio (1855-59); as U.S. secretary of the treasury (1861-64) helped develop the national banking system; chief justice of the U.S. Supreme Court (1864-73)

Charles Waddell Chesnutt (1858-1932), born in Cleveland; writer; one of the first black writers to gain recognition in America; works include the story collections *The Conjure Woman* and *The Wife of His Youth*; awarded the NAACP's Spingarn Medal in 1928

Arthur Holly Compton (1892-1962), born in Wooster; physicist; awarded the 1927 Nobel Prize for physics for his discoveries about the behavior of X-rays

James Middleton Cox (1870-1957), born in Jacksonburg; politician, media executive; U.S. representative (1909-13); governor of Ohio (1913-15, 1917-21); Democratic nominee for president of the United States (1920)

Harold (Hart) Crane (1899-1932), born in Garrettsville; poet; his epic poem, *The Bridge*, explored his vision of the symbols, myths, and hopes of the American experience

George Armstrong Custer (1839-1876), born in New Rumley; military officer; served in the Union army in the Civil War; engaged in Indian fighting (1867-76); killed while acting as commanding officer in the Battle of Little Bighorn

Clarence Seward Darrow (1857-1938), born in Kinsman; brilliant lawyer; defended over fifty accused murderers; noted for his participation in the famous Scopes trial, in which he defended a Tennessee teacher's right to teach the theory of evolution

Charles Gates Dawes (1865-1951), born in Marietta; lawyer, banker, politician; first director of the U.S. Bureau of the Budget (1921); in 1923, drew up the Dawes Plan to restore and stabilize the German economy in the aftermath of World War I; vice-president of the United States (1925-29); ambassador to Britain (1929-32)

Paul Laurence Dunbar (1872-1906), born in Dayton; poet and novelist; won popularity by combining humor, dialect, and a lyrical style; best known for his poetry collection *Lyrics of Lowly Life* and the novel *The Sport of the Gods*

Thomas Alva Edison (1847-1931), born in Milan; considered one of the world's greatest inventors; took out 1,093 patents in his lifetime for such inventions as the incandescent electric lamp and the phonograph

Harvey Samuel Firestone (1868-1938), born in Columbiana; industrialist; founder and president of Firestone Tire & Rubber Company in Akron

William (Clark) Gable (1901-1960), born in Cadiz; film actor; appeared in more than seventy films; best known for his portrayal of Rhett Butler in *Gone With The Wind*; won the Academy Award for best actor for his role in *It Happened One Night* (1934)

James Abram Garfield (1831-1881), born in Cuyahoga County; twentieth president of the United States (1881); U.S. representative (1863-80); was elected to the U.S. Senate (1880) but accepted the Republican party presidential nomination instead; was assassinated four months after taking office

John Hershel Glenn, Jr. (1921-   ), born in Cambridge; astronaut; first American to orbit the earth (aboard Friendship 7, February 20, 1962); U.S. senator (1974-   )

Benjamin Franklin Goodrich (1841-1888), industrialist; pioneer rubber-goods manufacturer; in 1870 opened a rubber-goods factory in Akron that eventually became the B.F. Goodrich Company, maker of automobile tires

Hiram Ulysses (Ulysses Simpson) Grant (1822-1885), born in Point Pleasant; eighteenth president of the United States (1869-77); illustrious Civil War general; in 1864 was named supreme commander of the Union forces; led the Union army to victory in the closing months of the war; after the war, was named General of the Army (1866); though he personally was honest, his two-term presidency was marred by political scandals

William Green (1873-1952), born in Coshocton; labor leader; president of the American Federation of Labor (AFL) (1924-52)

Zane Grey (1872-1939), born in Zanesville; novelist; wrote some sixty popular western-adventure novels, including *Riders of the Purple Sage*

Charles Martin Hall (1863-1914), born in Thompson; chemist, manufacturer, inventor; pioneered the aluminum industry in the United States after he developed the first practical aluminum extraction process

Margaret Hamilton (1902-1985), born in Cleveland; film actress; best known for her role as the Wicked Witch of the West in the 1939 movie *The Wizard of Oz*

Marcus Alonzo (Mark) Hanna (1837-1904), born in New Lisbon; businessman, politician; U.S. senator (1897-1904); influential supporter of William McKinley; served as McKinley's advisor and friend during McKinley's presidency

THOMAS EDISON

CLARK GABLE

ZANE GREY

MARK HANNA

WARREN HARDING

BOB HOPE

PHILIP JOHNSON

CHARLES KETTERING

Warren Gamaliel Harding (1865-1923), born near Corsica (now Blooming Grove); twenty-ninth president of the United States (1921-23); owned and edited the *Marion Star* (from 1884); U.S. senator (1915-21); as president he called for a return to "normalcy" after World War I, but his administration was involved in several scandals, notably the Teapot Dome affair, in which Harding's secretary of the interior accepted a bribe to permit private development of federally owned oil fields

William Rainey Harper (1856-1906), born in New Concord; scholar and educator; president of Yale University (1886-91); first president of the University of Chicago (1891-1906)

Benjamin Harrison (1833-1901), born in North Bend; twenty-third president of the United States (1889-93); grandson of President William Henry Harrison; U.S. senator from Indiana (1881-87); as president, he supported civil-service reform, protective tariffs, and reciprocal trade agreements with Latin America

William Henry Harrison (1773-1841), ninth president of the United States (1841); governor of the Territory of Indiana (1800-12); U.S. representative from Ohio (1816-19); U.S. senator (1825-28); served the nation's shortest presidential term when he caught a cold at his inauguration and died thirty days later

Rutherford Birchard Hayes (1822-1893), born in Delaware; nineteenth president of the United State (1877-81); Civil War general; U.S. representative (1865-67); governor of Ohio (1868-72, 1876-77); as president, withdrew federal troops from the South, ending the Reconstruction era

Woodrow Wilson (Woody) Hayes (1913-1987), born in Upper Arlington; fiery football coach at Ohio State University (1951-68); built Ohio State into a perennial football power

Robert Henri (1865-1929), born Robert Henry Cozard in Cincinnati; artist, art teacher; founded what became known as the Ashcan School of art, which focused on the realities of urban life

Bob Hope (1903-   ), born Leslie Towne; entertainer, film actor; moved to Cleveland at the age of four; one of America's best-loved comics; has appeared in movies, radio, and television

Philip Cortelyou Johnson (1906-   ), born in Cleveland; architect, architectural critic; one of the leaders of the architectural movement known as post-modernism

Charles Franklin Kettering (1876-1958), born near Loudonville; electrical engineer, inventor; invented the first electric cash register and the first electric automobile self-starter; cofounded the Dayton Engineering Laboratories Company (Delco) (1908); vice-president and director of research for General Motors Corporation (1920-47); cofounded the Sloan-Kettering Institute for Cancer Research in New York City (1948)

Maya Ying Lin (1960-   ), born in Athens; artist; designer of the Vietnam Veterans Memorial in Washington, D.C.

William Holmes McGuffey (1800-1873), educator; president of Cincinnati College (1836-39) and Ohio University at Athens (1839-43); helped found Ohio's common-school system; best known for his *Eclectic Readers*, popularly called "McGuffey Readers," which were widely used in the late 1800s

William McKinley (1843-1901), born in Niles; twenty-fifth president of the United States (1897-1901); U.S. representative (1877-83, 1885-91); as a congressman, won passage of the McKinley Tariff Act of 1890; governor of Ohio (1892-96); as president, he expanded United States territories overseas with the addition of Puerto Rico, Cuba, Guam, and the Philippines; assassinated by anarchist Leon Czolgosz

Chloe Anthony (Toni) Morrison (1931-   ), born in Lorain; writer; concentrates on the problems of finding a black identity in America's white-dominated society; best-known novels include *The Bluest Eye*, *Song of Solomon*, and *Beloved*

Paul Newman (1925-   ), born in Shaker Heights; film actor and director; best known for his roles in *The Hustler*, *Cool Hand Luke*, *Butch Cassidy and the Sundance Kid*, *The Sting*, and *The Verdict*

Jack William Nicklaus (1940-   ), born in Columbus; professional golfer; all-time leading money winner in professional golf

Annie Oakley (1860-1926), born Phoebe Anne Oakley Moses in Patterson; markswoman; sharpshooter with Buffalo Bill's Wild West Show (1885-1902); her showstopping stunts included hitting a dime in midair from 90 ft. (27 m)

Bernera Eli (Barney) Oldfield (1878-1946), born in Wauseon; race-car driver; popularized the sport in the United States when, in 1903, he became the first driver ever to reach the speed of 60 mph (97 km/h)

Ransom Eli Olds (1864-1950), born in Geneva; inventor and pioneering manufacturer of automobiles; built his first gas-operated car in 1896; founded the Olds Motor Works in Detroit, Michigan (1899) to produce his "Oldsmobiles"

James Cleveland (Jesse) Owens (1913-1980), athlete; grew up in Cleveland; starred on the Ohio State University track team (1933-36); in 1935, made the finest one-day showing in track history by setting three and tying one world track record; in the 1936 Olympics in Berlin, he disproved dictator Adolf Hitler's theory of Aryan "supremacy" by winning the 100-meter and 200-meter races and the long jump and ensuring victory for the 4x100-meter relay team

TONI MORRISON

PAUL NEWMAN

ANNIE OAKLEY

JESSE OWENS

RUFUS PUTNAM

WILLIAM T. SHERMAN

GLORIA STEINEM

CARL STOKES

Rufus Putnam (1738-1824), Revolutionary War patriot and Ohio pioneer; helped organize the Ohio Company of Associates (1786) to develop the western lands; founded Ohio's first permanent settlement, Marietta (1788); surveyor general of the United States (1796-1803)

Edward Vernon (Eddie) Rickenbacker (1890-1973), born in Columbus; aviator, airline executive; World War I flying ace; wrote *Fighting the Flying Circus* about his war experiences; president of Eastern Airlines (1938-63)

Peter Edward (Pete) Rose (1941-   ), born in Cincinnati; professional baseball player and manager; played with the Cincinnati Reds, the Philadelphia Phillies, and the Montreal Expos; manager of the Cincinnati Reds (1984-   ); in 1986 broke Ty Cobb's record of 4,191 hits to become baseball's all-time leading hitter

Constance Mayfield Rourke (1885-1941), born in Cleveland; historian; author of several books of historical interest, including *Trumpets of Jubilee, Davy Crockett,* and *Audubon*

Arthur Schlesinger, Jr. (1917-   ), born in Columbus; historian; special assistant to President John F. Kennedy (1961-64); won Pulitzer prizes for his presidential histories of Andrew Jackson *(The Age of Jackson)* and Kennedy *(A Thousand Days)*

John Sherman (1823-1900), born in Lancaster; lawyer, politician; U.S. representative (1855-61); U.S. senator (1861-77, 1881-97); in 1890 drafted the Sherman Anti-Trust Act and the Sherman Silver Purchase Act; secretary of the treasury (1877-81); secretary of state (1897-98)

William Tecumseh Sherman (1820-1891), born in Lancaster; brother of John Sherman; military officer; Union army general whose "scorched-earth policy" devastated the South

Steven Spielberg (1947-   ), born in Cincinnati; film director; has made a number of blockbuster films, including *Jaws, Raiders of the Lost Ark,* and *E.T.: The Extraterrestrial*

Edwin McMasters Stanton (1814-1869), born in Steubenville; lawyer, public official; U.S. attorney general (1860-61); secretary of war (1862-68); appointed associate justice to the U.S. Supreme Court, but died before taking office

Gloria Steinem (1934-   ), born in Toledo; author, women's rights activist; in 1971, helped establish the National Women's Political Caucus and the Women's Action Alliance; founder of *Ms.* magazine (1972)

Carl Burton Stokes (1927-   ), born in Cleveland; lawyer, politician; mayor of Cleveland (1967-71); first black elected mayor of a major American city

Harriet Beecher Stowe (1811-1896), novelist; lived in Cincinnati (1833-50); drew upon that experience for characters and incidents in her famous novel, *Uncle Tom's Cabin, or Life Among the Lowly*

Robert Alphonso Taft (1889-1953), born in Cincinnati; politician; son of William Howard Taft; U.S. senator (1938-53)

William Howard Taft (1857-1930), born in Cincinnati; twenty-seventh president of the United States (1909-13); U.S. circuit court judge (1892-1900); U.S. secretary of war (1904-08); as president, encouraged "dollar diplomacy" (federal government support for United States business investments abroad), enforced antitrust legislation, and supported constitutional amendments to allow an income tax and direct election of senators; Yale University law professor (1913-21); chief justice of the U.S. Supreme Court (1921-30)

Arthur (Art) Tatum (1910-1956), born in Toledo; jazz pianist; noted for virtuoso performances as a soloist and with his own jazz trio

Tecumseh (1768-1813), born near Columbus; Shawnee chief; spokesman for the Indians of the Ohio Valley; attempted to unite the eastern American Indian tribes against white settlers; sided with the British in the War of 1812 after losing the 1811 Battle of Tippecanoe

Tenskwatawa (1768?-1834), known as the Prophet; Shawnee religious leader; brother of Tecumseh; advocated returning to traditional ways; with Tecumseh, worked to unify the Indians of the Ohio Valley; defeated by William Henry Harrison in the 1811 Battle of Tippecanoe

Lowell Jackson Thomas (1892-1981), born in Woodington; news broadcaster; best known for his nightly radio news broadcasts (1930-76); narrated "Movietone News" (1935-52)

James Grover Thurber (1894-1961), born in Columbus; writer, illustrator, and humorist; managing editor of *The New Yorker* magazine (1927-33); his essays, short stories, and cartoons appeared throughout his life in *The New Yorker*; best-known works include the story "The Secret Life of Walter Mitty" and the collection *The Thurber Carnival*

Lillian Wald (1867-1940), born in Cincinnati; nurse, social reformer; pioneer in public-health nursing; pioneered the idea of public-school nursing

John Quincy Adams Ward (1830-1910), born in Urbana; sculptor; famous works include *Emancipated Slave* in Cincinnati and *Indian Hunter* in New York City's Central Park

George Washington Williams (1849-1891), lawyer, politician, historian; practiced law in Cincinnati; U.S. minister to Haiti (1885-86); scholarly works include *The History of the Negro Race in America*

HARRIET BEECHER STOWE

WILLIAM HOWARD TAFT

ART TATUM

TECUMSEH

ORVILLE WRIGHT

Orville Wright (1871-1948), born in Dayton; aviation pioneer; inventor (with his brother Wilbur) of the first successful self-propelled airplane; made the first successful flight in a self-propelled heavier-than-air craft, on December 17, 1903

Wilbur Wright (1867-1912), aviation pioneer; invented, with his brother, the first successful self-propelled airplane

Denton True (Cy) Young (1867-1955), born in Gilmore; professional baseball player; won more games (511) than any other pitcher; elected to the Baseball Hall of Fame (1937)

GOVERNORS

Edward Tiffin	1803-1807	Richard M. Bishop	1878-1880
Thomas Kirker	1807-1808	Charles Foster	1880-1884
Samuel Huntington	1808-1810	George Hoadly	1884-1886
Return J. Meigs, Jr.	1810-1814	Joseph B. Foraker	1886-1890
Othneil Looker	1814	James E. Campbell	1890-1892
Thomas Worthington	1814-1818	William McKinley	1892-1896
Ethan Allen Brown	1818-1822	Asa S. Bushnell	1896-1900
Allen Trimble	1822	George K. Nash	1900-1904
Jeremiah Morrow	1822-1826	Myron T. Herrick	1904-1906
Allen Trimble	1826-1830	John M. Pattison	1906
Duncan McArthur	1830-1832	Andrew L. Harris	1906-1909
Robert Lucas	1832-1836	Judson Harmon	1909-1913
Joseph Vance	1836-1838	James M. Cox	1913-1915
Wilson Shannon	1838-1840	Frank B. Willis	1915-1917
Thomas Corwin	1840-1842	James M. Cox	1917-1921
Wilson Shannon	1842-1844	Harry L. Davis	1921-1923
Thomas W. Bartley	1844	A. Victor Donahey	1923-1929
Mordecai Bartley	1844-1846	Myers Y. Cooper	1929-1931
William Bebb	1846-1849	George White	1931-1935
Seabury Ford	1849-1850	Martin L. Davey	1935-1939
Reuben Wood	1850-1853	John W. Bricker	1939-1945
William Medill	1853-1856	Frank J. Lausche	1945-1947
Salmon P. Chase	1856-1860	Thomas J. Herbert	1947-1949
William Dennison	1860-1862	Frank J. Lausche	1949-1957
David Tod	1862-1864	John W. Brown	1957
John Brough	1864-1865	C. William O'Neill	1957-1959
Charles Anderson	1865-1866	Michael V. DiSalle	1959-1963
Jacob Dolson Cox	1866-1868	James A. Rhodes	1963-1971
Rutherford B. Hayes	1868-1872	John J. Gilligan	1971-1975
Edward F. Noyes	1872-1874	James A. Rhodes	1975-1983
William Allen	1874-1876	Richard F. Celeste	1983-
Rutherford B. Hayes	1876-1877		
Thomas L. Young	1877-1878		

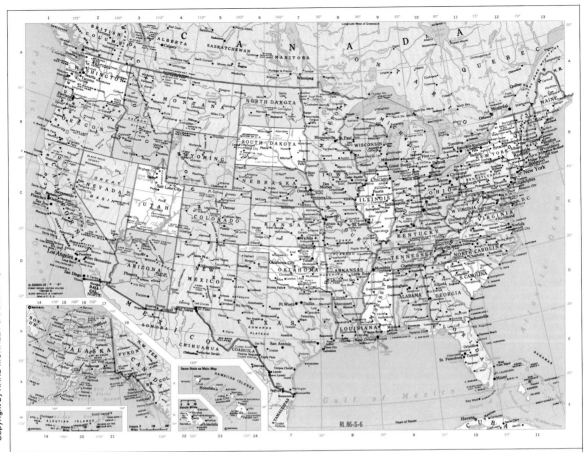

Topography

MAP KEY

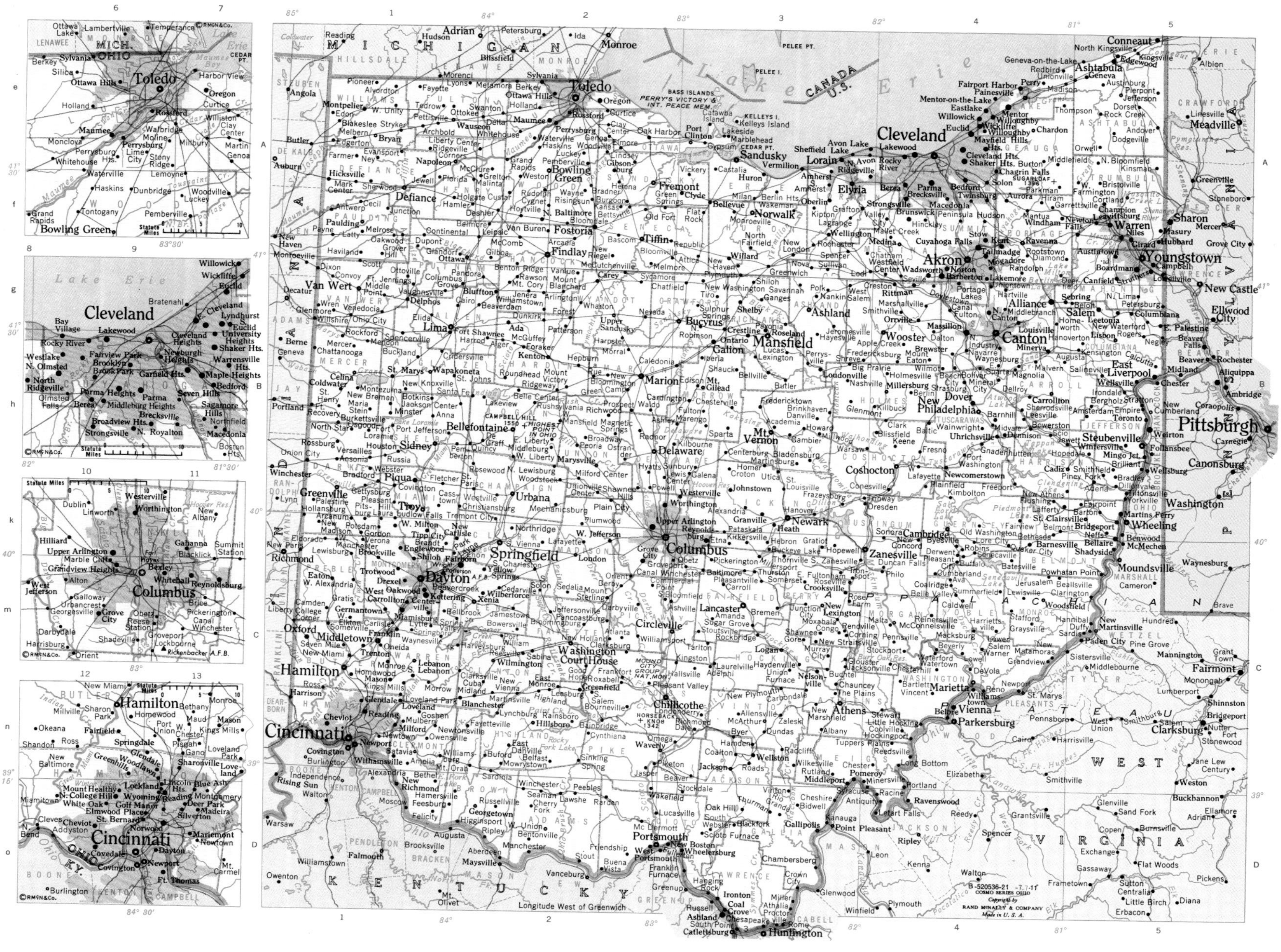
MICHIGAN
Lake Erie
CANADA
U.S.
PERRY'S VICTORY & INT. PEACE MEM.
INDIANA
KENTUCKY
WEST VIRGINIA
Toledo
Cleveland
Akron
Canton
Youngstown
Pittsburgh
Columbus
Dayton
Cincinnati
Springfield
Mansfield
Hamilton
CAMPBELL HILL 1550 HIGHEST POINT IN OHIO
Longitude West of Greenwich
B-520536-21 -7-7-11
COSMO SERIES OHIO
Copyright by RAND McNALLY & COMPANY
Made in U. S. A.

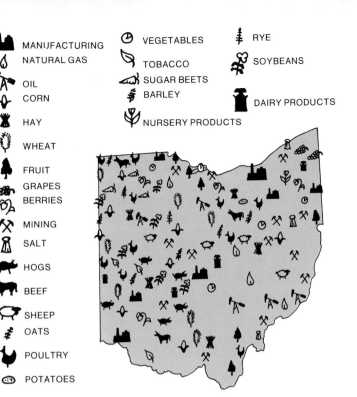

MANUFACTURING
NATURAL GAS
OIL
CORN
HAY
WHEAT
FRUIT
GRAPES
BERRIES
MINING
SALT
HOGS
BEEF
SHEEP
OATS
POULTRY
POTATOES

VEGETABLES
TOBACCO
SUGAR BEETS
BARLEY
NURSERY PRODUCTS

RYE
SOYBEANS
DAIRY PRODUCTS

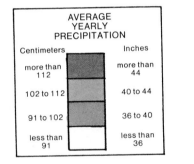

AVERAGE
YEARLY
PRECIPITATION

Centimeters		Inches
more than 112		more than 44
102 to 112		40 to 44
91 to 102		36 to 40
less than 91		less than 36

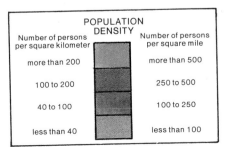

POPULATION
DENSITY

Number of persons per square kilometer		Number of persons per square mile
more than 200		more than 500
100 to 200		250 to 500
40 to 100		100 to 250
less than 40		less than 100

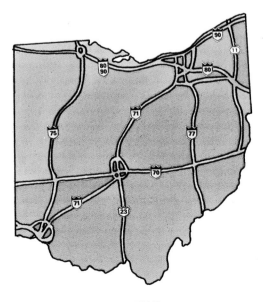

MAJOR HIGHWAYS

TOPOGRAPHY

5,000 m. | 2,000 m. | 1,000 m. | 500 m. | 200 m. | 100 m. | Sea
16,404 ft. | 6,562 ft. | 3,281 ft. | 1,640 ft. | 656 ft. | 328 ft. | Level | Below

Courtesy of Hammond, Incorporated
Maplewood, New Jersey

COUNTIES

The Ohio River and the Cincinnati skyline

INDEX

Page numbers that appear in boldface type indicate illustrations

139

Horseback riding in an Ohio park

142

Picture Identifications

Front Cover: The Columbus skyline and the Scioto River at twilight
Back Cover: The Ohio River at Cincinnati
Pages 2-3: Tuscarawas County
Page 6: The Ohio River at Gallipolis
Pages 8-9: Old Man's Cave Lower Falls in the Hocking Valley
Page 18: Montage of Ohio residents
Pages 24-25: The Great Serpent Mound at Serpent Mound State Monument
Page 30: An engraving from the early 1800s showing an emigrant wagon bound for Ohio
Pages 40-41: The Harrison farm at North Bend, Ohio, in 1840
Page 54: The Cuyahoga River at the Flats in Cleveland
Page 64-65: The State Capitol in Columbus
Pages 78-79: The Cleveland Museum of Art
Pages 88-89: Cincinnati and the Ohio River at twilight
Page 108: Montage showing the state flag, the state tree (buckeye), the state bird (cardinal), the state flower (scarlet carnation), and the state fossil (trilobite)

About the Author

Deborah Kent grew up in Little Falls, New Jersey, and received a bachelor's degree in English from Oberlin College in Oberlin, Ohio. She earned a master's degree in Social Work from Smith College School for Social Work. As part of her social-work training, she spent a year working in a Cleveland nursing home, where her elderly clients regaled her with memories of Ohio that dated back to the 1880s and 1890s.

Ms. Kent did social work in a New York City settlement house and taught children with disabilities in Mexico before she began writing full-time. She is the author of many novels for young adults, as well as several other titles in the *America the Beautiful* series. She currently lives in Chicago with her husband and their daughter Janna.

Picture Acknowledgments

Third Coast Stock Source: © Ed Kreminski: Front cover, Pages 8-9, 11 (left), 12 (left), 54, 95, 103 (middle left), 106, 121; © Eric Albrecht: Pages 2-3, 4, 18 (bottom right); © Tony Casper: Page 116

Shostal Associates: Pages 6, 24-25, 75, 91, 113; © Bernard G. Silberstein: Back cover, Pages 13, 68; © Gene Ahrens: Pages 64-65; © Paul Heiselman: Pages 88-89; © R. Glander: Page 100; © Karl Kummels: Page 103 (top left); © Steven L. Alexander: Page 104

Root Resources: © James Blank: Pages 5, 14, 72, 77, 138; © Paul R. Silla: Pages 12 (right), 70 (left); © Ian J. Adams: Page 15 (left); © Brad Smith: Pages 18 (top right), 103 (bottom); © Larry Hamill: Page 73; © J.C. Allen & Son, Inc.: Page 76

© **Jerome Wyckoff:** Page 11 (right)

© **M.L. Dembinsky, Jr.:** © Skip Moody: Page 15 (right); © Carl R. Sams, II: Pages 16 (left), 108 (cardinal)

© **Reinhard Brucker:** Page 16 (right)

© **Larry Hamill:** Pages 18 (top left), 20

Cameramann International Ltd.: Pages 18 (bottom left), 69, 70 (right), 71, 74 (both photos), 78-79

Photri: Pages 22-23 (all photos), 94, 128 (Hope), 130 (Sherman), 131 (Tatum); © Frederick Francis: Page 117

© **Eastern National/Mound City Group National Monument:** Page 27 (all photos)

The Granger Collection: Pages 30, 32, 35, 37, 40-41, 50, 56, 84 (right), 130 (Putnam)

New-York Historical Society: Page 36 (left)

© **Smithsonian Institution:** Page 36 (right)

© **Joan Dunlop:** Page 38

Ohio River Museum: Page 43

Gartman Agency: © Michael Philip Manheim: Page 18 (middle left); © James P. Rowan: Pages 45, 93

Historical Pictures Service, Inc., Chicago: Pages 46, 53, 82 (left), 127 (Edison, Hanna), 128 (Harding), 129 (Oakley), 131 (Tecumseh)

Library of Congress: Page 47

Cincinnati Art Museum, Subscription Fund Purchase: Pages 49, 84 (left)

Courtesy of the Cincinnati Historical Society: Page 57

UPI/Bettmann: Page 59

Wide World: Pages 60, 62, 82 (top and bottom right), 125 (Anderson), 126 (Darrow), 127 (Grey), 128 (Johnson), 129 (Morrison, Owens), 130 (Steinem, Stokes), 131 (Taft), 132

All-American Soap Box Derby: Page 87

© **Jerry Hennen:** Page 92

Journalism Services: © Mike Kidulich: Page 97

© **Richard Lewis:** Pages 98, 141

SuperStock International: Pages 103 (middle right), 127 (Gable), 129 (Newman)

Ohio Department of Natural Resources: Page 108 (buckeye tree, trilobite)

Ohio Division of Travel & Tourism: Page 108 (carnations)

Cincinnati Reds Public Relations Department: Page 118

© **James P. Rowan:** Page 119

Courtesy of the Ohio Historical Society, Campus Martius Museum, Marietta, Ohio: Page 123

National Gallery of Canada, Ottawa: Page 125 (Brant)

National Portrait Gallery, Smithsonian Institution: Pages 126 (Chase, Dawes), 128 (Kettering)

Western Reserve Historical Society: Page 126 (Chesnutt)

Sophia Smith Collection, Smith College: Page 131 (Stowe)

Len W. Meents: Maps on Pages 92, 94, 100, 103, 106, 136

Courtesy Flag Research Center, Winchester, Massachusetts 01890: Flag on Page 108